The
Spell
of the
Shell

The Spell of the Shell

MARTHA KEELING HODGSON

HAWTHORN BOOKS, INC.
Publishers/NEW YORK

THE SPELL OF THE SHELL

Library of Congress Catalog Card Number: 74-15641

ISBN: 0-8015-7016-6

1 2 3 4 5 6 7 8 9 10

To Pat

Contents

Acknowledgments and Author's Note

Although the words conchologist and malacologist are bandied about in the following pages I make no claim to be either. I am a beachcomber who loves shells for their beauty and for the interest in seeking them in their natural habitats. Such knowledge as I have acquired of them has been gained on their breeding grounds from native fishermen, from the Conchological Society of Great Britain and Northern Ireland, from other collectors, and from a variety of books and magazines too numerous to mention. I owe a special debt to Roderick Cameron for his fascinating books *Shells, The Golden Haze,* and *Viceroyalties of the West;* to the late Miguel Covarrubias for his authoritative work on Bali; to T. V. Bulpin for his book *Islands in a Forgotten Sea;* and to the National Geographic Society (U.S.A.) for information drawn from articles published in their magazine.

Many of the photographs of our shell collection and the objets d'art were taken by my step-granddaughter Sara Heaton whom I thank warmly for her skill and patience. Photograph on page 20 is by courtesy of the duke of Bedford. Photograph on page 25 is by courtesy of the duke of Richmond and Gordon. Photograph on pages 22–23 were kindly lent by the Viscount Boyd of Merton. Photograph on page 18 is reproduced with permission of the Victoria and Albert Museum, and photograph on page 161 is reproduced with permission of the British Museum of Natural History. The photograph on the front cover of the jacket is by the courtesy of Anne Bolt. The embassies of France, Mexico, Indonesia, and the office of the Fiji High Commission have all kindly put photographs at my disposal. All other photographs were taken by me and by my husband, Patrick.

Lastly I want to express my gratitude to the late Geoffrey Wethered for his help and interest in this book in its early stages, and above all to thank my husband and beachcombing partner, Patrick, not only for opening to me the mysterious world of the shell but for transporting me to those distant and exotic islands where the humble mollusks create their own strongholds of such ingenious and moving beauty.

I have referred to the seashells throughout by their common as well as Latin names. An appendix at the end of this book lists both.

The
Spell
of the
Shell

1 Nucleus

A collision occurred between my life and that of the mollusk at a time when I was almost totally committed to the fine arts of mankind rather than to those of nature. I recall the moment of impact precisely, for it was one of those significant events, unrecognized as such at the time, which continues to discharge concentric and ever-widening rings from a seemingly inexhaustible nucleus. The occasion promised to be one of almost unmitigated boredom. A great country house in Devonshire, Arlington Court to be exact, was being formally handed over to the National Trust by the high sheriff, and speeches of mutual congratulation and regard droned on interminably. The mayor and aldermen, robed in broadcloth and sable, and an invited audience perspired and shifted uneasily in the steaming drawing room of the late Miss Rosalie Chichester, the donor. My eye roved beyond the congested scene into the deserted reaches of a classically columned hall. It remained there, riveted upon a cairn of variegated seashells, which, transmitting rays of amber, amethyst, rose, citron, and sepia, gleamed and glowed prismatically in the late afternoon sun. "Then felt I like some watcher of the skies when a new planet swims into his ken." Closing words to the ceremony there must have been, but I did not hear them. I swam out of my chair and into that hall in a trice—whatever a trice may be—where I kenned and kenned.

"Pray help yourself!" A minnow of a curator stood at my elbow, smiling thinly and kindly. I picked up a shining miracle

1

of a cowry shell, covered in tortoiseshell flecks, and held it to my ear. High tide somewhere. "Do you mean I may choose one of these?"

"Take as many as you like. Take a bowlful. These are seconds, and we are giving them away to our guests as mementos."

That was the beginning. When I got home I piled the shells high in a cream and gold Leeds bowl and set them in the center of the dining room table where they remain to this day, shining in the perfection of their unself-conscious beauty, objects of envy and fascination to a diversity of guests—whose reaction to them, however, is strangely predictable. One after another the visitor will lift a shell from the bowl, hold it up to his ear and turn it in the palm of his hand to savor the luster. "It is enough to make you believe in God," he will say, so often that we have come to wait for it.

This confrontation with the world of the mollusk not only satisfied my pleasure in proportion and rhythm but aroused my curiosity. I was next to be seen in the Chelsea Public Library, embroiled with textbooks on conchology and malochology, the sciences of the shell and of the occupants thereof respectively. But when I further pursued the subject through the galleries of the British Museum of Natural History, the immensity of the subject gave me pause. A busy widow of some years standing, I was already three times a grandmother. Also I was preoccupied with the problem of how to make a second marriage with a man who lived, somewhat inconveniently for such purposes, in Buffalo, New York. Conchology would have to wait.

This proposed marriage with Patrick Hodgson, my future husband, was not quite so unlikely an event as might be supposed. We had known each other since we were in our teens, and although our adult lives had been spent on different continents, a tenuous thread of communication had never been entirely severed. When after forty years chance threw us together again, we therefore had solid, if somewhat inaccessible, ground under our feet. In the interval Pat had become senior partner of a great firm of lawyers in the state of New York and during the war had served as general counsel to the United

States Navy in Washington. I had married a member of Parliament with a safe London seat, done a stint in the WRNS (I fancied the tricorn hat), and spent a merry year as lady mayoress of the city of Westminster. But the world of fine arts and of architecture, of museums, of the great country houses and their contents, of the National Trust and Georgian Group were what preoccupied my first husband, Edward Keeling,[1] known as K, and me. David Eccles [2] says K was the pioneer ecologist, and I put it on his tombstone. We rarely found time to look out of the window except at some park by Capability Brown or a garden by Humphrey Repton.

On the other hand Pat, my intended husband, in his spare time was a hunter (Indian version), a bird-fancier, a trainer of gun dogs, and a big-game fisherman and, so to speak, was already out of doors and rarely spared a glance at what lay within. Each knew this aspect of the other. But what I didn't know about him was that over the years a passing interest in conchology had developed into a passion, and that he had gradually assembled a near perfect collection of shells from the beaches of west Florida. From time to time Pat accuses me of having married him for this collection, when I crisply cross-charge him with having married me for my red hair.

Pat first got hooked on the shores of Saipan and Leyte during the attack on Japan, where shells like gems glittered on the assault beaches, disregarded by all but Pat, who put some in his briefcase or haversack, or whatever general counsels carry. His favorite sport has always been fishing for tarpon and snook so, after the outbreak of peace, his holidays were spent among the Ten Thousand Islands, off the Everglades of Florida, which include some of the finest shelling beaches in the world and certainly the most agreeable conditions. When the fish were not running, Pat occupied himself by upgrading his shell collection. He had found all the shells himself, learned the local names, habits, and habitats of each specimen and, except for the best, which were displayed in a glass-covered

[1] Sir Edward Keeling
[2] The Viscount Eccles, PC, KCVO, then minister for arts

3

coffee table in Buffalo, kept them stowed away in shoe boxes.

While by flying visits, telephone, and cable we were groping our way towards some compromise between living in Buffalo, New York, and London, S.W.1., I had reason to visit Guernsey and thus the nearby little island of Herm. Herm's shores are starred over with a thousand thousand shells, minuscule, as befit the occupants of its tiny beaches, but brilliantly hued; flame, pearl, violet, orange, black. On his next exploratory visit Pat was electrified at a sight of a couple of dozen match-boxes on a tray, each covered by me in vivid shades of velvet and encrusted with shells from Herm. Herm? He had never heard of it. Marco or Boca Grande, Sanibel or Captiva, islands all; these were his stamping grounds, of which I, in turn, had never heard. The shells that he had found there over the last thirty years compared, he declared, in size, variety, and beauty with any of those that adorned my dining room table and now also filled my drawing room grate. (Piled high and lit from below, this arrangement is at least as pleasurable and much less trouble than a log fire but needs the backing of a sound system of central heating.) This mutual disclosure of suitable addresses at which to collect shells seemed to provoke a clinching process. Inperceptibly the last barriers were sur-mounted. We found ourselves indisputably wed, for better for worse, on Christmas Eve in a snowstorm, with a three-month honeymoon yawning before us at the most inclement time of year.

Digging our way out of a snowdrift one evening, we decided —having just seen the film of that name—to go round the world in eighty days but to use different methods. The odds seemed to be in favor of hitting the right season for at least some of our objectives—big-game fishing, for instance—and seeing the Taj Mahal at dawn and, we realized when we examined the itinerary of the S.S. *Caronia*, to which we pro-posed to entrust ourselves, of enlarging and extending our shell collection. For among other destinations we were due to spend several days at such shelling centers as the Cayman Islands, Mexico, the Philippines, Bali, Japan, Ceylon, and on the shores of the Red Sea. Pat's mother declared no marriage could survive so prolonged a honeymoon, and Pat himself was at first averse

We decide to spend our leisure exploring the shell centers of the world, but do not normally look as tidy as this. Photograph by Patrick Hodgson.

to a cruise at all. He had already experienced several. The passengers, he said, disembarked at daybreak and long before noon tended to pass out in low bars, having developed an allergy to temples, native dancing, and local crafts. This forecast proved to be an accurate one but did not affect us. Beaches were within reach of every port, and at each one we slipped away to the shore, often finding a child or a fisherman to guide us and sometimes hiring a boat. Natives would materialize carrying bowls of local specimens they had found in their nets or on the reefs while searching for food or digging for bait. Sometimes they took Pat out fishing, and on one occasion he caught a magnificent marlin, which, as usual, he released. Once, off Mexico, he was absorbed in playing a sailfish until he saw the *Caronia*, with me on board, sailing past him bound for Honolulu. Another time he caught a shark from waters in which I had just been enjoying a tranquil and naked swim.

In the short time available we did not find rare shells, but we saw enough to whet the appetite. An ambition and a plan to carry it through germinated almost simultaneously in both our minds. It was to spend our leisure exploring the shell centers of the world and to assemble a collection of the rarest specimens by all means available. We would set aside in our house, wherever it might be, a room in which to enjoy their enchanting beauty. Through books, or perhaps through some learned society, we would master knowledge of the nature and the habits of the creators of that beauty.

By the time the dream had begun to harden into reality, Pat was already practicing law in London, and we had established ourselves in Onslow Square within sound of a church bell chiming the hour, an owl hooting from a lilac tree, and horses' hooves returning to Knightsbridge barracks. The cook's bedroom had been transformed, by turquoise silk walls, long mirrors, Ionic columns, a Blue Period Picasso and a Chinese birdcage for a lamp, into a setting, we hoped, worthy of our expanding collection. The cook was put out to grass. Here Pat's Florida collection held pride of place. He still remembers on which beach and at what phase of the moon each shell was garnered with his own hand, and this is the only "pure" section of our so-called museum. The rest has been assembled as opportunity presented itself. Sometimes we could not help feeling a bit nettled when collectors, after examining our treasure, would inevitably end with the same question: "I suppose you haven't got a glory of the sea?" Of course we hadn't. Who has, except the curator of one of the great natural history museums? But in 1969, after years of speculation concerning its habitat, a glory of the sea was found alive in deep water near Guadalcanal. Later this specimen came up for auction at Sotheby's and we got it, a superb shell, a golden and white marvel of grace. We also used this simple, if expensive, method to acquire a glory of Bengal. This white and burnt sienna cone of incredible elegance, covered by a design of snow-covered Alps receding into a conic whorl at the apex, is one of the rarest shells in the world. Even its existence was unknown until recently.

Other shells of particular interest are those whose rarity depends upon some abnormality of growth, or upon their being deformed by some disease peculiar to a certain region; as

We found shells so beautiful that we established a room in our flat in which we could simply look at them. Photograph by Patrick Hodgson.

for example the Niger cowry, a shell found only at New Caledonia in the South Pacific, its swarthiness due to a mineralogical condition that exist nowhere else; or the *Cypraea moneta rostrée* (rostrée means distorted), a brilliant yellow cowry with a hump like a camel, found occasionally off Nouméa. The rest have been bought in shell shops all over the globe, bargained for with beach boys and guides on the spot, wherever that spot might be, dived for by children for coppers, bartered for in exchange for ball-points, plastic earrings, lipsticks, and rolls of lavatory paper in Bali, in Ceylon, at Pemba to the south of Mombasa, and combed from nets of the shrimp fleet at San Francisco.

And once I received a magnificent gift. Out of the blue a letter arrived from John o' Groats in Scotland, in which a woman, having fallen asleep during a broadcast by me on the BBC, wrote to ask what I had said I did with the shells once I'd found them? I had received many such letters—mostly from those who owned a small collection that they hoped to sell at a large price—but there was a sympathetic quality about this downright letter that drew from me a full response. For one thing, she obviously loved shells herself. I replied that we found shells so beautiful that we had established a room in our flat in which we could simply look at them, and that we had recently joined the Conchological Society of Great Britain and Northern Ireland that we might learn about their creator with a small c. I told her that I passed on what I learned to a number of children, starting them off only with a few shells at a time in order not to surfeit them; I said I also gave these children a simple textbook and exhorted them to refer to the shells from the start by their Latin appelations. I described a conchological meeting we had attended that same afternoon in a hall lent to us by the Linnæan Society, where my goddaughter Athene English, aged fourteen, had been held spellbound for an hour by a lecture that dealt exhaustively with the three shades of excrement— black, brown, and beige—of a certain land snail in Northumbria, the slug *Vertikulatis*. She had sat under a portrait

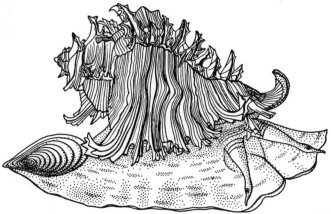

Top, *Chicoreus ramosus* Linné. Right, *Helix (Cepaca) nemoralis* Linné. Drawings by J. Webb. Courtesy The Conchological Society of Great Britain and Ireland.

of Darwin who in 1859 had first expounded in that very room his theory of the origin of species. I added as a postscript that I owned a studio where I both made, and taught others to make, shell collages, designed to let the natural charm of the shell speak for itself rather than to create a realistic picture. This autobiographical outpouring was received in silence, and I forgot all about it. A few months later, glancing down from the balcony, I noticed a personable young man unloading a strangely shaped assortment of boxes on my door-step. Investigation revealed a superb collection of seashells from Mauritius in their original containers, assembled by my correspondent's deceased great-aunt towards the end of the last century. These were now being bestowed upon me as a gift.

But the shells we value most are those sought, oft in danger and in woe, oft also in the dark and on an empty stomach, and found after strenuous exertion on some inaccessible reef or beach. Incidentally, shells for a collection should be secured alive, for only in this condition will they retain their brilliant sheen. Dead shells gleam deceptively while they lie in glassy water, lit by a blaze of sunshine, but they assume a chalky dead texture when they dry out. Dealers in shells have been known to try to restore such specimens by tinting and spray-ing them, but such profanity is instantly detectable by the ex-perienced shell fancier.

It is my habit to comb the reefs grasping a parasol, saturated with oil, loaded with gear, and bent double, calling aloud on St. Anthony of Padua to guide me towards some particular treasure—a checkerboard clam, perhaps, or a sunrise tellin—he does a fine job several times a day in locating my reading glasses, and I have come to depend upon him. My tendency is to cover too much ground at a glance, rolling my eyes from side to side as if executing exercises for the ophthal-mologist. Pat, on the other hand, in as near a state of nature as decency permits, relies upon a gimlet eye that looks deeply into drifts of shells and among the sea wrack. Asking nought of heaven, he cuts an all-seeing swath around his advancing feet, often finding shells that I have missed, his head bowed like Rodin's "Thinker." Pat is less afraid of sea monsters than I am, and in general less squeamish. Sharks, for instance, give me nightmares, while Pat believes it when told they are harmless. I am also averse to such dumb friends as the stinging starfish, the stingray, the stonefish, the jellyfish, the poisonous sea snake, and a family of venemous cone shells with disarming names like tulip, textile, and geographic, in the gathering of which strong men have died. Then, I am positively allergic to the squid, whose embracing arms sometimes reach fifty feet in length; the octopus; the man-eating barracuda; the sea urchin with quills like lancets; and worst of all, the moray eel, who, once he has closed his jaw on a questing hand cannot unlock it even if he would. So there you would be, you and the moray eel, till death did you part.

Most but not all of these monstrosities, however, are so-journers on tropical reefs, and for this reason the call of the west coast of Florida with its gently shelving beaches is the one to which I most readily respond. Never mind about the condominium on Marco Island where Gritts's tackle store once stood, the supermarket where eagles used to nest in a monu-mental oak, or the discotheque instead of a sanctum for the Holy Rollers. For tiny islets still glisten with newly cast-up shells; huge beaches unroll, white as if under a fresh fall of snow; and ospreys soar into the air with threshing fish gripped in their talons.

Only a few weeks ago we were beachcombing down Hurricane Pass near Marco. "St. Anthony!" I cried aloud into the peacock blue sky, plumed over with clouds of fluffed-out cotton wool: "What about a junonia this morning?" Now the junonia is one of the most highly prized shells in Floridian waters—an ivory volute dappled with purplish brown flecks. A once-in-a-lifetime shell. In his thirty years of shelling, in fact, Pat had found but one and a half, and, he observed dryly that I was asking rather a lot of St. Anthony—and I a heretic, too. And so indeed it proved.

However, at daybreak next morning, aware that the tide was racing in, I roused Pat with the suggestion that we should take the boat to a certain stretch on Little Marco Pass. Still half asleep, we beached her on the lee shore of a point fast disappearing under a swirling current. It so happens that I am something of an expert on knots and confound Pat with the ease with which I tether up our craft with sheepshanks, running bowlines, and clove hitches, a relic of salad days in the Brownies. On this morning, however, I leaped over the side, leaving Pat to tie up as best he might, and sprinted along the sand to the tip of the promontory. The sea was ruffled by a high wind so, bending double as if seeking some object I knew to be there, I advanced thigh-deep into the turbulence. Rolling out to sea on the sandy bottom I saw a single shell. It was a perfect junonia. I lunged after it, but it trundled serenely on out of reach. Fully clad and wearing a new watch, I threw myself head first into the sea and managed to grasp it. The Koh-i-noor diamond itself could not have been a more gratifying find. Up to the neck in water, with dripping hair, I sat holding it to my lips looking, Pat said, like a beached mermaid. I hope St. Anthony heard my psalm of thanks.

The excellence of shell collecting lies in the fact that it satisfies so many needs at once. It provides adventure, connoisseurship, aesthetic satisfaction, and probably, but not necessarily, foreign travel. And it is so good for your waistline. Also the eye sharpens, the bare foot hardens, and all tensions evaporate. Besides, I know of no keener pleasure than the moment of confrontation with some fine shell, yearned for and sought for and as familiar, through illustrations in the textbooks, as one's own reflection in the mirror. Also it is for young and old, male and female, novice and expert, and can be joyously shared with another, yet at the same time remain a private adventure. The collector of shells can be in good or ill health. He can assemble them in the open air and arrange, study, and classify them at his own fireside. There can also be infinite variations and permutations, some of which I will mention briefly.

After Captain Cook's return from the South Seas in 1771, the craze for shells and everything pertaining to them mounted almost to a mania. The revelation of the tropical shell had already broken like a thunderclap over the heads of European arbiters of taste. Goldsmiths set shells for them in precious metal, while artisans created every form of folly; for instance, I own a sewing box made from a pair of huge violet mussels mounted in ormulu and a turban shell made into a miniature

11

fire engine containing a crystal scent bottle and drawn by a silver-gilt horse. Jewel caskets, mirrors, picture frames, étuis, and figurines positively dripped with shells. Porcelain manufacturers produced superb dinner services decorated with them, artists painted pictures of them, sculptors sculpted them, and cabinetmakers devised delightful vitrines in which to exhibit all this sophistry. Mrs. Delaney, a celebrated wit at the court of George III of beloved memory, decorated her privy with them.

12

After Captain Cook's return from the South Seas in 1771, the craze for shells and everything pertaining to them mounted almost to mania. For instance, I own a sewing box made from a pair of huge violet mussels mounted in ormolu; also, a turban shell made into a miniature fire engine, containing a crystal scent bottle and drawn by a silver-gilt horse. Photograph by Sara Heaton.

Our collection of natural shells is augmented with eighteenth-century shell snuffboxes, and it has been the greatest fun running these rarities to earth. They crop up in the Portobello Road and in the Burlington Arcade; in Christie's or Sotheby's and in junk shops; in the Brighton lanes, in antique fairs, and in a very few private collections. They vary from common shells mounted in simple metal settings—these often inscribed with such sentiments as "Be True" or "My Own" or "As a Gift—'tis Valuable"—to the rarest of shells set in twenty-carat

13

Our collection of natural shells is augmented with antique shell snuff-boxes. . . . Reading left to right, back row, textile cone, mounted in silver with shell section on lid, c. 1730; tiger cowry, mounted in ormolu, mother-of-pearl lid, signed RT and dated (Richard Tudor, Dublin, 1786), c. 1820; silver-mounted whelk, horseshoe-shaped lid, c. 1800; tiger cowry, mounted in gilt and pinchbeck, c. 1770; hump-backed cowry in mounted silver by Samuel Green, Cork, 1760. Middle row, Tent Olive, mounted in gold, Louis XV, c. 1770; sundial, mounted in gold, David Thomas, 1967; striped bonnet, eighteen-carat gold, David Thomas, 1968. Front row, miniature tiger cowry, silver-lined with gilt, formed as a vinaigrette, c. 1780; miniature double shell, mounted in silver, c. 1770; and egg-shaped mother-of-pearl box, mounted in brass, c. 1850. Photograph by Sara Heaton.

gold, exquisitely chased and bearing the mark, date, and city of the maker. Intermediately, there are boxes set in tortoiseshell or mother-of-pearl, in copper, silver, or pinchbeck, and these add a gleam of metal to shelves sometimes overloaded with the products of carbonate of lime.

Owners of stately homes of Europe, and particularly those in England, next contracted a fever for shell rooms, temples, and grottoes, a passion now shared by Pat and me. Guidebook in hand, we sleuth through deepest Somerset, North Wales, South Cornwall, or Grosvenor Gardens in London, in which a pair of shell pavilions adorn the French garden behind General Foch. First in the field in 1627—as you might expect

Dollhouse made from shells, roof made from red admiral butterfly wings, garden made from dried seaweed, c. 1805. Photograph by Sara Heaton.

Shell "sailor's letters" from Barbados. The rare octagonal mahogany frames close into boxes. Kindly lent by Dr. Christian Skiff. Photograph by Sara Heaton.

Nautilus shell cup, mounted in gold, set with gems, c. 1770. Victoria and Albert Museum, London.

if you put faith in the doctrine of heredity—was an ancestor of the present duke of Bedford. So quick off the mark was the noble owner of Woburn Abbey that loads of tropical shells, which later flowed into England like lava, came too late for his particular folly. The entrancing jungle of mermen and maids, dolphins, Neptunes, and starfish that riot over the walls and ceiling of his entrance hall are largely formed from the rather boring ormer shell, a native of Jersey.

A unique circular building, À la Ronde outside Exmouth, is one of our favorites. The rooms radiate from a central octagonal hall above which towers a ravishing shell gallery, decked in designs of birds, roses, crowns, and coats of arms, the work in 1798 of the ladies of the Parminter family whose descendants still own this curious house; the drawing room walls and ceiling, for instance, are decorated with feathers. Once my first husband, K, and I were invited to lunch there, because the reigning Misses Parminter, elderly maiden ladies, were planning to give the house to the National Trust. What I believe are known as the usual services, such as the front doorbell, the heating system, and the plumbing, seemed irremediably broken down and, wearing overcoats, we ate cold pork off the kitchen table as if at Wuthering Heights. In West Quantoxhead two footmen of Lord St. Audries spent their free time in building a Gothic shell grotto in the garden. Enormous shells are suspended from the ceiling like stalactites, interspersed with spirited and aspiring vines, carried out in cockles, mussels, and whelks. The poet Alexander Pope's grotto at Pope's Grove in Twickenham is dramatically illuminated but is rather disappointing, most of the shells having been prized out of the rock as mementos by devotees visiting the shrine of the Master.

In this century, Alan and Patsy Boyd[1] have maintained the tradition by building themselves a gazebo in their garden at Ince Castle in Cornwall. Octagonal in shape, its walls, ceiling, and floor are overlaid with formal patterns of shells, while the doorknob consists of a single tiger cowry. Still in this century but in Palm Beach, Bunny Dupont,[2] the trans-

[1] The Viscount and Viscountess Boyd of Merton
[2] Mrs. Nicholas Dupont

Shell grotto, entrance hall of Woburn Abbey, home of duke of Bedford, c. 1627.

In West Quantoxhead two footmen of Lord St. Audries spent their spare time in building a Gothic shell grotto in the garden. *Evening Post*, Bristol.

(a)

Shell grotto (gazebo) built by Viscount and Viscountess Boyd of Merton: a. exterior, b. interior, window, c. interior, wall, d. marble floor, e. ceiling. Photographs by Mark Lennox-Boyd.

22

(b)

(c)

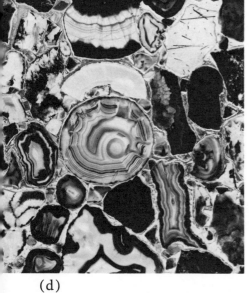

(d)

(e)

atlantic version of these enthusiasts, lives in a crystal and marble equivalent of Neptune's Halls. Coral arrangements flower in niches: shell collages, vitrines of fine specimens, and shell sailor's letters from Barbados adorn her walls. Even her dinner service, fragile as the Argonaut itself, is an adaptation of this perfect mariner's design, carried out in the eighteenth century in shell pink Wedgwood. On the lawn lie two halves of a giant clam that Bunny picked up somewhere on her travels, which she now uses as a footbath. They must be four feet long and weigh at least as many hundred pounds. She found it somewhere on her travels and brought it home by air.

Back again in England, there are too many fascinating temples and pavilions to enumerate, so I shall describe only one more, our particular fancy, the teahouse at Goodwood House, built in 1739 by the duchess of Richmond and Gordon and her two daughters. It took them seven years to cover the walls with elegant swags and urns and cornucopias in South Sea shells and to lay a mosaic floor made from the teeth of the duke's deceased racehorses. He also is said to have lent a hand, but intermittently.

Although this book was planned as an account of how we formed a shell collection and what we did with it, it has grown to embrace a somewhat wider field. So the following pages describe not only the regions to which our obsession led us but also how we gradually and sometimes painfully acquired a firsthand understanding of the mollusk itself; of the territories in which it breeds; and of people whose horizons are bounded by the elements and to whom volcanoes, hurricanes, typhoons, and tidal waves are a constant hazard.

In some places that we attained after considerable expenditure of spirit as well as of the pocket, we found hardly any shells at all. But we encountered instead fascinating human beings; wild creatures of the sea, sky, and woods; and much history in the raw. We saw whales, eagles, and Charles Lindbergh; temples, rites, firewalking, and feasts; double rainbows, sacred waterfalls, and a volcano in full eruption. I am reminded, as I look back upon the sculptured and scrolled grace of the rocks and waves that encircled like garlands the islands from

It took them seven years to cover the walls with elegant swags and urns and cornucopias. The teahouse at Goodwood House, built in 1739 by the duchess of Richmond and Gordon and her two daughters. Photograph by Martha Hodgson.

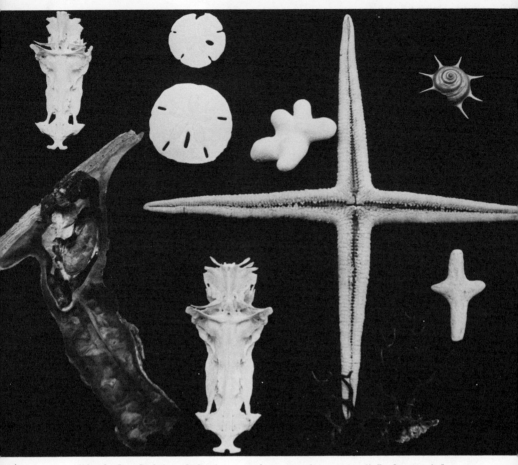

"And the Spirit of God moved upon the water." Left to right, top row, crucifix bone of Fayuum carp, sand dollars with Easter lily and the five wounds of Christ, sculptured infant in coral, four-pointed starfish, triumphant star shell; bottom row, hammer oyster, crucifix bone, thorns for the crown, crucifix in coral. Photograph by Sara Heaton.

which we drew our treasure, of a mosaic made in 1182 at Mon Reale Cathedral, Sicily. It depicts the Almighty in the act of creating the ocean, and below it is inscribed: "And the Spirit of God moved upon the waters." It must have been at this point, I think, that he looked and "saw that it was good."

26

2 Mexico

Before the destination for our first full-scale operation is settled, we begin to prepare ourselves for it by haunting the meetings of the Conchological Society. The idiom is at first difficult to grasp. ("Run off," I read in my notes, for instance, "is satisfactory but soil creep is rapid," or "In the field progress in the dark is circuitous but at dawn the slug moves in a straight line.") Also, all mollusks are referred to familiarly by their Latin names, giving the impression that the meeting is being conducted in ancient Rome. However, we manage to grasp the basic structure of the world of the mollusk, and before taking off for first base I shall describe it briefly.

The word "mollusk" means literally "soft-bodied," since its Latin root is *mollis* (soft). This body is usually, but not always, encased in a hard shell composed of carbonate of lime. *Concha* is Latin for shell, hence conchology. There are five main classes of mollusca, the most primitive being Amphineura, which consist of the chitons or coat-of-mail shells that carry on their backs eight crescent-shaped disks and have a flat muscular foot. The second class, Scaphopoda, includes all those shells that resemble minute elephant tusks. Next comes Gastropoda, the sea snail of the ocean, the owner of a spiral shell or a conical one like the limpet, and a leathery foot. Then follows Lamellibranchia, the class that includes all the bivalves, such as oysters, clams, and the beautiful classical scallop. Finally, there are the Cephalopoda, of which the best-known examples are the cuttlefish, the squid, and the wonderful chambered nautilus with its ingenious spiral shell. So once the general life-style of the mollusca has been grasped they fall naturally into their correct compartment and, before you realize it, Latin names for them are popping out of the subconscious as if known from some previous incarnation on the shores of Sybaris.

We opt for Mexico for our opening venture because both of us have ulterior reasons for wanting to go there. Pat, after a nostalgic examination of his stuffed sailfish languishing in the wine cellar, is to be seen rigging up various fishing rods and assembling a whopper of a tackle box—all of which, incidentally, he loses at Heathrow before we start. My curiosity about Mexico is already unbounded. It had been aroused by an exhibition of pre-Columbian art, which came to London at the end of the last war. Unsuspectingly I had swanned into the private view at the Tate Gallery to be met by an impact that struck me like a punch in the solar plexus. With a pounding heart I looked around for somewhere to sit other than upon the floor. Ignorant of the significance of the exhibits, I began feebly to focus upon the two nearest to me—both of them gods with built-in sacrificial vessels. One was a nightmare tiger, all bared teeth and fangs, the other an evil potbellied presence with semihuman features, engulfed in serpents. Each had a pit between the shoulders to accommodate the sacrifice. And the sacrifice, you may ask? Human hearts, no less, torn from the flesh of living victims with an obsidian knife. These and a succession of equally grisly deities discharged so potent and disgusting an aura that they instantly generated in me a determination to explore the land that begat such monsters and to probe into the reason for their creation. So what with a promise from the textbooks that seashells by the thousands flourish both along the Pacific and the Gulf coasts and a prospect of big game fishing as well as a newly opened anthropological museum, we decide to make for Mexico City and play it by ear thereafter.

The wheels to perfect this plan having been set in motion, we roll in looking as if we had spent the night in prison. Our hotel is seven thousand feet above sea level, plus a hundred or so more because we are roosting in the clock tower on the roof, the clock of which has inopportunately stopped—which way do we put our watches, forward or back?

Presently, somewhat restored by a siesta and a highly spiced dinner, we gravitate towards the main square, the Zócalo, where the cathedral and palace are incandescently aglow with golden floodlighting. Here we somehow intermingle with a Mexican family on its way to the ballet and find ourselves packed in with it in the private box of the minister of the interior. Perhaps our host is the minister of the interior. The violent aboriginal rites—those of the Yaqui tribe are supposed to have surfaced with the dawn of the ever-rising sun—and the erotic Spanish dances with Mexican overtones that follow induce a sense of disorientation. Or maybe it's the altitude, or the all-Mexican menu at dinner? The finale, however, is the most revealing. In this sequence of dances the Aztec god, Huitzilopochtli, with his own blood animates bones from which he creates man. He has, it seems, need of man to worship him.

"Self-centered!" I hiss into Pat's ear. "All he wants man for is to eat him." Pat shakes his cheeks at me: "Hush." Doomed but adoring, poor man struggles on, stuck between sun and moon, light and night, good and evil. And what's he got to offer in return for this supreme gift of life? The fruits of the earth, the sacrificial blood of beasts, his creative powers? Not enough! His very life? That's it! These jolly gods of theirs can only be placated by the ultimate sacrifice—the living hearts of strong young men and of golden girls.

"You won't know me, Senora Iturbe, but I'm a friend of the so-and-so's . . ." Elaborate explanations prove to be unnecessary and are cut short by . . . "and so I will fetch you, Martha, and your husband—how is he called, Pat?—at two o'clock, and you will have lunch with Luis and me. About seashells, I can tell you all."

She can indeed. Tiechi Iturbe, a name picked, fortunately indeed, from our Mexican list, has a fine collection of shells herself and is thus familiar with their lares and penates. They gleam and glow on shelves in the patio where we consume a gargantuan meal that lasts until five o'clock.

29

Now then, they ask us briskly, what do we want to see? Or are we more interested in politics? Or history? Of course, we know already about King Montezuma and the Spaniard Cortes and the conquest that destroyed the Aztec civilization? Well, afterwards it seems that Mexico was ruled by viceroys from Madrid until 1810, when the Mexicans threw the Spanish out. Napoleon III next had a go, offering the Mexican crown to the Austrian Archduke Maximilian and guaranteeing his protection with French troops. The poor man was executed as an "invader" three years later. A dictator followed, Porfirio Díaz, who survived until 1911 but was displaced after failing to break up the great private estates. This reform is now well under way, Luis adds wryly, and I remember a reference to his cattle ranches somewhere in the north, probably his no longer.

On the way home we are confronted by the unsymmetrical pile of the Chapultepec Palace which, built on the site of King Montezuma's summer palace, looms starkly above the ahuehueete trees beneath which the monarch himself must have meditated, for they are said to be a thousand years old. Here the unlucky Emperor Maximilian and his Coburg consort, Carlotta, hastily moved from the quarters provided for them in the Zócalo, which had stood vacant for at least forty years. The first night of their reign was spent there upon the billiard table because the state bed was infested with bugs. We are guided through a series of ornate anterooms into an overstuffed throne room by an Indian, a man both of imagination and of a philosophical turn of mind.

"Stand here, Senora. From this window the empress would watch for the carriage that would bring her husband home at night. That is, if he came home at all." For Maximilian struggled in the bug-ridden palace with the chaos of Mexico all day and sought relaxation by night in arms other than Carlotta's. "See that avenue of chopos and alaos trees, Señor? The emperor planted it as a triumphal route, but before they got to the height of his spurs—phut—he was dead. And under this canopy, dressed in their coronation robes, Maximilian and Carlotta received homage and oaths of loyalty from the nobilities." The scene is not hard to imagine, for over the throne hangs a portrait of the doomed couple, radiant in full monarchal glory. Significantly, however, a vitrine under it contains a pair of Carlotta's tiny, once white, satin boots, a broken mother-of-pearl comb, and a moth-eaten feather fan.

The final exhibit is a painting of the empress, now bareheaded and wearing a sensible serge dress and an inscrutable expression. Is it one of foreboding, of defiance, or a mask disguising the insanity to come? It was painted only a month before she fled to Europe, to madness, to widowhood, and finally to a solitary death at the age of eighty-six in the castle of Bouchart, back in Belgium where she started from. No grizzly detail of Maximilian's execution is spared us; it is described by the guide with a certain exasperated relish. For the deluded emperor obviously meant well, but his ideas were liberal—too liberal for the conservative element that had originally offered him the throne and was the first to repudiate him. But what of it? In revolutions many heads roll, Maximilian's among them. Our guide glances up at the somber painting of the empress. "Carlotta should never have left him to die alone. But in the end, Senora, she lost her nerfs."

I too look up at the enigmatic Carlotta and recall a description I read somewhere of her eyes: "Dark in the center and about the edges an unholy green."

" 'Ello, 'ello, Martha?"

"Yes. I mean si."

"This is Norma Redo, the sister-in-law of Tiechi. Today it is your turn to lunch with us and also Pat?"

What could be more effective than the Mexican bush telegraph method?

The Redo establishment is not unsuitably named "Versailles" and must be about as convenient. In a salon dark with teak furniture, heavily upholstered ancestors gaze down from massive frames upon a scintillating party. Our host, Diego Redo, is Tiechi's brother and like her has kaleidoscopic eyes, glittering between blue and violet, fringed with gorgeous eyelashes. Norma, his wife, is a neat, petite, and widely informed ash blond. The minister for this is announced, the professor for that. The secretary of state for something is followed by several beautiful children who leap into the room and out again. Princesse de someone. The Swedish ambassador. Marita. The conversation, in faultless English, ranges from politics and anthropology—on which the chic Marita is somewhat unexpectedly writing a book—to ranching and sport. The fare is pure Mexicano, and I steer a careful course between the pork and the pimento.

Advice is conflicting about the best shelling area. "Cozumel," declares our hostess firmly. This is an island off the coast of Quintana Roo in the remote south. "Baja California." insists Tiechi, which could hardly be farther north; it is the peninsula looking like a crumpled sock that straggles down the top letf of the map. "If I were you I should go to Acapulco and be comfortable," murmurs monsieur le ministre. "Cozumel," intones Norma like a Greek chorus. "It will be hot, the water also, and shells lie upon the beach the size of my handbag." One glance at her vast reticule clinches it. Cozumel is out. We settle for Baja California and kind Tiechi darts to the telephone to book us into the hotel, concerning which there is total agreement. It is the most civilized hotel imaginable. None of them, it transpires, has actually stayed in this elysium, but all envy us the prospect. "And the gulf is renowned for its fishing; for shelling. . . ." Well, no one really knows, but the beaches stretch out into infinity.

That question settled I give my attention to my neighbor, harassed professor who is somewhat off his oats owing to the student riots that are dislocating his college. The problems in Caycayan University coincide with those being endured by professors everywhere, and I can only nod in helpless sympathy. From him, however, I glean two pieces of information for which I have since searched reference books in vain. Firstly, the concept of zero was grasped as early as the fourth century by the Mayan civilization, and the sign for this spectacular discovery was actually a cowry shell. Secondly, stout Cortes, no less, with his wild surmise come true, lies buried close by in the modest chapel of a hospital founded by him, the Jesus Nazarene.

I'm startled. "Why isn't he in the cathedral?" The professor explains that Cortes died in Spain but under a provision in his will his body was buried in Mexico, where it was several times abducted by zealous supporters to save it from desecration. Finally he was entombed secretly in this obscure hospital in the Pino Suarez, where after luncheon we discover the grave of this incredible prodigy set in a wall marked by the most unpretentious of plaques.

Our aircraft, having been wished a blessed journey through the loudspeaker, speeds off for several hours over vacant plateaus and plains before a glitter of water preludes the appearance of a chessboard of squat dwellings set in a dusty depression—our objective, La Paz. Here we are to transfer to a midget plane. We cram in. An obese couple with corresponding luggage are stuffed in behind us, followed by a slip of an Indian with three crates of whisky. The congested scene is impassively surveyed by an outlandish-looking pilot, Sebastiano. His sole comment before climbing in is, "We are overloaded." Nevertheless, we stagger off the ground, which is of ocher clay seamed with jagged cracks and stippled with grey scrub and cacti the height of space rockets. Presently the land rises sharply and we skim over one saw-edged volcanic ridge after another. I close my eyes and wish I hadn't come. My theory is that air is for breathing and flying for the birds, and it is some years now since I was a bird. When I reopen them we are circling a wisp of airstrip that originates on the beach and runs obliquely up a hill that acts as a brake. We land with a clank of whiskey bottles.

We have been sustaining ourselves with anticipation of the delights awaiting us in "the most civilized hotel imaginable." Wet swimsuits, we were told, will be spirited away and returned dry within the hour. Nightgowns will be pressed daily, evening clothes laid out, and service with a smile can be taken for granted. But either conditions here have suffered a sea change or we are in the wrong hotel. The bath water is cold. There is a minimum of drawer space and no hooks. The bedside lights do not work, and there is no telephone. A reconnaissance discloses the news that the sea is ice cold, the fish are not running, and no shells are in evidence. As we glance through the window at the weird terrain to which our exertions have led us, we dissolve into tears of laughter. Suddenly all the

33

lights fuse. (Ha, ha, ha!) A sharp wind has sprung up that rattles the shutters, which won't shut. How much wiser—not to mention warmer—it would have been to have gone, as we had at one time intended, to Antibes.

The marlin fishing boats are just due in, so in excellent spirits we scramble over the rocks to meet them. No luck today. (Ha, ha, ha!) A school of goose barnacles, like silver rosebuds with coral stamens, have been marooned in their hundreds against a breakwater by the falling tide. Ocean craft are bedeviled by these stalked crustaceans, which grow in artistic sprays on their hulls, causing so great a loss of speed that they frequently have to repair into dry dock to have their bottoms scraped. As I have neither before nor since seen such a barnacle I gather the lot in my skirt, which to this day reeks of decomposing denzeeps (short, believe it or not, for denizens of the deep).

Dinner is transformed into an unexpectedly energetic operation by the authoritative wail of the tango. Eight or ten Mexicans with firm tenor voices and a galaxy of guitars thread their way in between the candlelit tables. There is no room to dance, but this troubles no one. Couples locked together are dancing where best they may, swaying and swooping among the waiters, out on the balcony, on the landing, and into the kitchen. The impression that South American dancing is not for me is dispelled by a Mexican about half my height. Perhaps it is the local tequila in my veins that responds to the tempo. Unimpeded by his heavy spectacles, we are soon glued together cheek-to-cheek, dipping, stamping, and curvetting. Pat, sitting among a group of friendly Californians—leaving, of course, tomorrow—is debilitated by laughter each time we glide past, and he receives a haughty Mexican glare from me, which he surely misinterprets, for he laughs the louder.

Throughout the night the Pacific thuds, sucks, and roars. "In cross section," I learn from a book of reference, "a wave momentarily forms the pattern of a logarithmic spiral, with the crest curving in and under to place its apex at the center of gravity. This figure, perpetually repeated by waves as they mount the beach, forms the identical curve that you find in the cone, conch, cowry, snail, and nautilus shell." Good gracious, does it really? I can hardly wait until tomorrow to watch these tactics.

It turns out to be a morning unfit for boating but suitable for apex-observing and for shelling. Equipping ourselves with stout shoes, gardening gloves, nets, and a stick for probing, we turn our faces eastward. A furlong from the hotel, long snakes of sea vine with succulent leaves begin to thread the blond sand. Elongated bones gleam among the sea wrack. Disintegrating crustacea and dorsal fin, sea fan, clumps of uniola (a form of sea oat), and tufts of wiry grass twine themselves into weird primeval designs. The material garnered from this stretch of shore is eventually incorporated into a John Piperish shell picture of leafless trees caught in a shrieking hurricane, against an indigo sky, slate water, and ocher earth. It is entitled *Mexico Remembered*.

Wherever water meets land exactly, the same convolution occurs. I've always taken breaking waves for granted, but now I find myself watching the process with attention. Each wave is built up by the backwash of the one before it, until the moment comes when the advancing wave can climb no higher. Undermined by the undertow, it curves forward and collapses on the shore. It is doing its logarithms, just like the book says. I watch, charmed, feeling like Einstein discovering relativity. Rather disappointing, somehow, after all the fuss. It must be less simple than it sounds.

Keeping at a respectful distance from all this turmoil, my attention is diverted by a striped snail with head and horns extended, promenading down a cleft in between the rocks. As I stoop to watch him an explosion of waves occurs in my left ear, and I find myself up to the armpits in water. Outraged, as well as endangered by the undertow, I limpet onto the nearest rock until the water recedes, leaving me running with red rivulets from a new poncho. Who said the ocean knew its logarithms? It must have mislaid its logbook. However, the sun now comes out with a shout and in five minutes I'm dry as a biscuit. Pelicans, gulls, and men-of-war glide low overhead, plopping into the water and taking off again, the whole enterprise requiring a surprising amount of exertion. Occa-

sionally a plane buzzes over and alights on the airstrip, throwing up a plume of sand.

Transferring my attention to the shells that spangle the shore or cling to trails of bladder wrack and tangleweed, I brood upon the hundred thousand different species already known and named, each of which, infinitely various and unendingly strange, is precisely adapted to its own particular life-style. Those, for instance, that feed on the surface are as thin as rice paper, the better to float on the ocean face; those that prefer to burrow in the seabed are heavy as lead. Others anchor themselves to rocks and take a snack off passing plankton, while yet others propel themselves through the water to dine off laggard prey. Each develops its own particular wheeze with which to attract and attack its victim and to defend itself.

It has long puzzled me how creatures with so rigid an exterior can nevertheless increase in size. Our museum in Onslow Square contains a number of "growth series" showing the same shell at different stages of development, each specimen as hard as rock.

Growth series of *Murex
radix* Gmelin. Photograph
by Sara Heaton.

The key to their ability to expand is the "mantle," a sensitive sheath that secretes carbonate of lime from which the shell gradually evolves, hardening into the shape dictated by its peculiar needs and by the color and content of its surroundings. The two forms of creation with which we are mostly concerned are the univalve or snail type, which is the possessor of a foot, a head with eyes, and a mouth; and the bivalve, which consists of twin shells interlocked by intricate hinges, as in the oyster or clam. The univalve originates in something called the nucleus, from which it spirals outwards in a pattern of growth based upon a precise mathematical law: the diameter of a coiled tube will grow in exact proportion to its length. The spiral grows only at the nucleus and, turning over on itself, increases in size but keeps its original shape. A bisected shell shows the amazing diversity that can develop from a marriage between a curve and this simple formula. The nucleus, in fact, itself differing endlessly, endlessly produces different variations of the same dynamic spiral. A comparison could be drawn with the small number of notes in music which, in different combinations, produces shall we say, Stravinsky's *Symphony of*

37

Psalms or Beethoven's Concerto. Leonardo da Vinci borrowed this spiral theme for his famous corkscrew staircase at Blois, and so did the Mayan architect who designed the tower of Chichén Itzá in southern Mexico.

The days pass in a variable procession. For short periods bursts of blinding sun emerge between bands of lowering cloud. An abrasive wind laden with grit drives the whitecaps close inshore, while ferocious-looking waves crash against the terrace wall, throwing up ramparts of spray. No one with any sense would venture into such a cauldron, and no one does. We compensate with a dip in a pool on the terrace, attained by a flight of steep stone steps, Late Sacrificial in architecture. This pool lies in deep shade and is fed from an ice-cold well. No one swims here either, and we only once.

Marlin and sailfish are beginning to run again, and Pat disappears at early cockcrow (they crow all day here) with Jesus, the skipper of a well-found craft called *White Otter,* and some sportsmen who have arrived in one of the air taxis that buzz across the sky at all hours and dot the fields around the airstrip like birds in bright spring plumage. From one emerges a couple looking like an advertisement in a travel brochure. They are blond and bronzed, with toothpaste smiles and matched luggage: John Carmack and his wife Anne. The unlikely element in this visit is that they are searching among the famished cattle and hovering vultures for a nice plot of sickly yellow desert upon which to build a bungalow. While surveying their projected site, I notice an ominous trail across the sand, which I indicate to the would-be vendor. "This has been a rattlesnake," he says genially after a brief inspection. "Many, many rattlesnakes here. Also copperheads and corals. All very poisonous. Please to be very careful. Also," he adds as an afterthought, with a glance at my bare feet, "we have the gila monster." This dumb friend is a miniature dragon—an outsize lizard—about two feet long, enclosed in iron casing, and armed with a lethal bite.

The fishing boats are sighted at sundown, the *White Otter* flying a blue pennant to show that a sailfish has been caught. I pray that the catcher is Pat, and so it proves. It is a corker;

An abrasive wind laden with grit drives the whitecaps close inshore, while ferocious-looking waves crash against the terrace wall throwing up ramparts of spray. Baja California Sur, Mexico. Photograph by Martha Hodgson.

nine feet long and weighing one hundred and six pounds; wonderfully and fearfully made, with a slim blue and silver body, a cobalt blue sail, delicately tapered fins and tail and startled circular blue eyes. It is the second-largest one ever caught in these waters. Looking modest and pink, Pat arranges to go out tomorrow after marlin, leaving me to investigate the shore.

Westward from the hotel the coast runs in a bracelet of tiny bays before opening out into an immense curving beach. Exact timing is needed to round each headland successfully. I narrowly scan each cliff of advancing water as it wallops down on the shore and rushes foaming madly up the beach. A violent suck back of rolling shale follows, leaving a few seconds clear in which to nip around the point into the next bay. Pat is somewhere among the whitecaps earnestly in pursuit of marlin and, as I examine the gulf for a trace of his craft, I am astonished to perceive a large cow with tapering upright horns swimming briskly shoreward. At first I cannot quite believe I am seeing what I see. Only when it begins to scramble through the shallows do I step prudently behind a rock, for I am not at all sure that this visitation is not a bull. In so doing I almost collide at knee height with a pelican who, motivated no doubt by similar misgivings, is also pushing off, for what else may not emerge in the wake of this maverick? —and there may not be room for all.

A precipitous track ascends the rock face behind me, which on all counts seems more desirable than life in a cove with a maddened sea cow. As it zigzags upward I must confess to giving a passing thought to my bare feet, the rattlesnake, and the gila monster, but nothing more alarming materializes than tiny lizards that dart for cover and black butterflies that flicker over cushions of rock roses. The climb gets tougher towards the top. "Perhaps," I reflect, spread-eagled over a chasm with one foot stuck in a cleft, "I should engage in enterprises more suited to one already three times a grandmother." But I scramble somehow onto a verge at the summit, which commands a view of the adjacent bays.

A battered tramp ship is moored offshore, towards which a scarlet rowboat is toiling, towing behind it six violently protesting bullocks lashed to the stern by the horns. On arrival they are winched aboard, either half-drowned or bellowing forcefully. My visitor in the cove is the one who got away. A herd of cattle stands passively in the shallows, tolerantly watching their struggling comrades and unaware that their turn is coming. At the foot of the cliff, among a knot of tethered horses and a flurry of lurchers, a group of cowboys in showy shirts, long, slashed chaps and spurred boots is swigging rum and shucking clams. Beyond them a majestic bay stretches into infinity, a Paul Nash scene in dove grey, oyster, and off-white punctuated by blanched bones and driftwood. Here the waves, in tranquil mood, are murmuring gently, already spent.

Presently, underlying a thin line of advancing dust, I hear the drumming of hoofs. The cowboys are approaching like a cavalry charge. A glance round reveals not a shred of cover and no alternative but to stand my ground. Bucking, yelling, and flourishing their sombreros, they divide and pass, leaving me petrified—as was no doubt their intention. The chase along the shore is to celebrate the dispatch of the final contingent of bellowing bullocks, and they rip onward and vanish into the rosaniline and auroral distance.

Next morning we are early abroad in glittering sunshine, the sky and sea viridian, the whitecaps still crowding the rocks and flinging up ramparts of spray. Anne Carmack, in a shocking-pink bikini with her long hair floating on the wind, and John, a bronze sculpture in Mexican pants, are sitting radiantly on the projected site of their bungalow playing gin rummy. They might be in the garden of Eden but well after the Fall. Endearing and ornamental though they are, we gaze upon them with misgiving for John, who is only forty-two, told me last night that Anne is his fifth wife.

We turn westward and Pat soon establishes himself at what he supposes to be a safe distance from the surf and begins to cast. He has not so far experienced the strangely irresponsible behavior of the Pacific at its margin, and he advances confidently to the water's edge. "Stand further back," I advise unwisely, "or you'll get knocked flat." Pat assumes the expression of an American gentleman in receipt of advice on a matter upon which his wife is not entitled to hold an opinion. Advancing several paces into the curling surf he makes a series of expert casts. The next time I glance up he has disappeared, but his head presently emerges from a receding bank of foam. After this he is lost to me among a group of fishermen high up on some rocks like miniature Alps, snowed over with guano, but even here the gods do not bless his rod, for the only thing he catches is a squid.

Immediately below our hotel is a cove that we have not investigated. A plethora of miniature shells lies here in glistening patches: dusky cones, iridian bubbles, wine red mussels, tiny key limpets lined with celadon green, horn shells and turkey wings the size of a grain of rice, and baby jingle shells —ebony, silver, tangerine, and amber.

Presently a conic whorl, a half-grown volute, steps briskly forth from my bag in search of leg room and ripples evenly along my walking stick. He is equipped with an extended feeler, a siphon, two long horns, tiny eyes, and a large leathery foot upon which he makes good time towards journey's end. At a touch, however, everything withdraws and he takes a toss into the sand. His foot, which was first out and last in, carries upon it a hard disk, called the operculum, that exactly fits the aperture of the shell. He is thus sealed in behind an impenetrable doorway so long as he is alive to hold it in position.

I stretch out contentedly among the windrows of shells, which glitter on the sand like tiny gems, while pelicans and ospreys sail overhead and cormorants brood upon a row of posts. How often we range the wide world over—well, a mile or so up the coast each way, anyway—in search of variety, success, or satisfaction—only to find it under our noses, back where we started from! The now famiilar crash of water interrupts these musings. I seize my shell bag and clutch my hat as a surge of water rushes up the beach and retires again, carrying with it my bath towel and *Spanish in Six Easy Lessons*. Just one easy lesson on the tactics of the Pacific Ocean is all I ask.

Meanwhile the hotel has been invaded by a convention of American Junior Chambers of Commerce. They are clean-cut, crew-cut, and in enviable health, particularly in the region of the vocal cords. Following a night punctuated by splashes and yells from the pool, outbursts of hilarity as they barge into the wrong bedrooms and a nocturnal croquet match, we decide to take off for Mazatlan on the mainland.

The effect of our Captain Oates's exit is rather spoiled by the discovery that the seats booked for us at La Paz were on a "plane that left yesterday." However, a two-hour flight that starts in the opposite direction to our objective brings us eventually to Mazatlan, all of thirty-five miles from La Paz as the vulture flies. We clip-clop off in an araña—a surrey with a fringe on top—into the old town, where, along the sea brim, stretches a white Spanish colonial inn studded with bottle green shutters and balconies. Within its galleried patio bloom oleander, bougainvillea, bamboo and rubber trees, and one soaring palm that seems to challenge the very sky. Umbrellas and tables are arrayed in emphatic shades of tangerine and

We clip-clop off in an araña. . . . Mazatlán, Sinaloa, Mexico. Photograph by Patrick Hodgson.

peacock, braziers glow beside each group of chairs, and a tramp in a deerstalker hat is sitting on the steps playing a violin.

In one corner of the patio is lodged a seafood joint, El Shrimp, jazzed up with paper flowers, photographs of celebrities, and fishing nets, and packed with locals at all hours. The waiters sing throatily at their task, frequently interrupting it to dance or to select a victim down whose throat wine is poured from a distance of two feet from a flagon with a long spout. As one orchestra succeeds the other, the displaced one adjourns outside to entertain the diners in the patio, so that both bands are blasting off together.

Awaiting a table on the first evening our attention is riveted upon a remarkable figure sitting alone on the steps. Her thin, high-bridged nose and topaz eyes, fringed with black eyelashes like broom bristles, are set in a waxen face. An ash-blond rope of hair hangs to her waist, and she is clad in a black sweater, stretch pants, and long white boots with spurs. Presently she clashes off under an archway into the street but reappears as we rise to go into El Shrimp. Wound round her body and interlaced with one another are two ten-foot snakes, a python and a boa constrictor. With rearing heads they ripple and

43

undulate in ashen and cinnamon coils, pouring themselves over her arms to hang down in heavy loops. She handles them as easily as a couple of feather boas.

"Do you know that girl?" I ask the head waiter when I have recovered from the shock.

"But yes, Senora, her name is Nicola."

"Is she Mexican?"

"Assuredly no, Senora, she is from Bath—is it?—in England."

"Where on earth does she get those snakes from, Carlos?"

"Always she keeps two in her car. In her flat, many more. With one she sleeps in her bed. But excuse me, Senora, I must speak with her; the manager does not welcome them here."

I doubt if they would be welcome in Bath, England, either.

The three islands of Las Gaviotas, said to be cuckoo lands inhabited by unicorn, phoenix, minotaur, and snark, lie in a tempting crescent a few miles offshore. A boatman to take us there has so far eluded us. "Today, alas, all the boats are out, save this one, Senor, which is in need of repair. . . ." or else the owner is at a bullfight or a funeral, or the tide is wrong, or it is a saint's day. However, we finally corner a grimy beachboy and his boat and, accompanied for some reason by a guide, half-Jewish and half-Irish, Shane by name, we potter off between banks of steaming mud into the open sea. We make for the middle island of the three that, in a dropping tide, are all becoming accessible to one another on foot. The sand, in bars of pale and somber gray, pale and deep ocher, deep brown and off-white, remind me of Bedouin carpets. The coves boil with fish; strange birds whir out of the scrub uttering melancholy croaks. The shore is covered with sultry-looking Aztec clams in checkerboard designs, with cup-and-saucer limpets and some black-tipped murex shells. Scattered fragments of crustacea suggest that certain slapdash characters have blithely discarded their shells, their segmented antennae, even their very limbs, and are presumably elsewhere growing them anew. It is not clear what Shane's function on this expedition is intended to be, nor how he came to be included in the party, for he knows nothing of shells and cares less.

He is, however, loaded down to the scuppers with breezy confidence and miscellaneous information, much of which subsequently proves to be incorrect. "O Erin! O Israel! All is not Gospel that thou dost speak." He suggests, however—and, avoiding his swivel eye on the beach next morning, we follow the suggestion—that we should cross the straits to yet another island, the Isla de Paulo.

We beach our boat here opposite a huddle of huts so primitive that it's hard to reconcile them with the gleaming skyscrapers in full view on the mainland that lies beyond the village. Strings of naked tousle-headed children and an occasional adult swathed in a coarse blanket shadow forth from the undergrowth. "Concha," we say—loudly, I fear, as if they were deaf, for they are known to speak only Nahuatl, the language of the indigenous Indian. Their gestures indicate that, although we are on the right track for somewhere, shells are to be found only by diving. We skirt a settlement behind which blows a cannabis field from which the island draws its supply of marijuana. An ancient figure of indeterminate sex plucks a spray as we pass and threads it through my buttonhole. High in a tree sways a huge boa constrictor—one of the family, we are assured by signs, whose function it is to keep down the rats. It is a relief to attain some mud swamps on the lee of the island, where we are rewarded by some dark, mottled starfish, like Van Gogh chrysanthemums, and an occasional sand dollar, which, as it dries, turns crisp as a biscuit. This singular creature appears to have five scars that encircle a lily etched on one side and a poinsettia on the other. A legend tells of the Easter lily, the Christmas poinsettia, of the five wounds of Christ, and of the five tiny doves of peace within, which drop from the creature when you break it open. I make great use in my flower pictures of these mothlike little symbols, which are in reality its teeth.

We are about to turn back when the miracle occurs. Resting upon the black mire as lightly as a pod of honesty is a perfect double royal comb Venus, the collector's prize of Mexico. Pat sees it two seconds before I do, making it forever his. This shell is a brittle bivalve arrayed in alternate stripes of white and lilac; a double line of fine cutlasslike spikes, twelve in the

A perfect double royal comb Venus, the collector's prize of Mexico. Isla de Paulo, Mexico. Photograph by Sara Heaton.

outer row, five in the inner, run from the apex of the shell to the rim. It is a poem of precision, balance, and beauty. Indeed, Georg Rumphius, an eighteenth-century Dutch naturalist, prized it so highly that he once offered a thousand pounds for a specimen. Pat makes it known that he is open to a similar offer from me.

Since the first touch of my foot on Mexican soil I have been subconsciously preoccupied with the problem of the early priesthood, whose beliefs created a cannibalistic godhead; with the noble Montezuma, the high priest and last of the Aztec kings; and above all with the fascinating Hernando Cortes, the instrument of their destruction. So many riddles remain unsolved that before long we are back again in Mexico City sleuthing the trail through the marble halls of the Anthropological Museum. This is arranged with such telling method and simplicity that the myriad questions that crowd into the mind are answered visually. Through the eyes of the monarch Montezuma we see his fabulous capital city, Tenochtitlan, and follow the chronicle of its downfall and that of the whole Aztec civilization at the hands of Cortes and his handful of conquistadors. A model of Tenochtitlan, set in the midst of five protective lakes approachable only by causeways five miles long, makes intelligible Cortes's awe when he first glimpsed it from the encircling heights. It shimmered as "if it were of sapphire stone, like the very heaven for clearness." Within these gleaming walls lived a million souls, three thousand of them in the royal palace alone, serving the king and his family.

For some years Montezuma had been haunted by catastrophic dreams and portents. It was predicted that on a certain day in the Aztec calendar Quetzalcoatl, the Toltec god, would return in glory to avenge his expulsion and extinguish the Aztec nation. By an uncanny coincidence, this fateful day, April 2, 1519, was the precise date on which Cortes, with a modest assembly of troops, priests, and some horses—animals never before seen in Mexico—disembarked where Vera Cruz now stands. Here he camped for some months, assessing his chances of conquest and meanwhile winning the confidence of certain Indians hostile to the Aztecs. Eventually the host labored over the mountain ranges towards Tenochtitlan, a trip that took eleven weeks. Girded for a bloody affray, they advanced into the royal city. To their stupefaction, they were ceremoniously welcomed by a cortege of nobles and warriors led by the king himself and his entire family. The Spaniards were loaded with gifts, encircled with garlands, and magnificently lodged in a palace adjoining the king's. Cortes of course, had no inkling that he was being received as the reincarnation of a god.

Encouraged by this aggressive reception, Cortes's actions became increasingly bold. First he commandeered the royal treasury, which included a solid gold sun seven feet in diameter, a great silver wheel, Montezuma's emerald the size of a goose's egg (which later appeared in the French crown but vanished during the Revolution), the sacred Aztec calendar carved with zodiaclike signs, and scepters, miters, bracelets, masks, and necklets, all of gold and encrusted with gems. It also included a coffer containing eight hundred seashells, tribute from a coastal tribe. Cortes's next move was to imprison Montezuma himself as a hostage against his own safety. To this the Aztecs reacted violently and assaulted the palace where Montezuma lay incarcerated. Convinced by priestly prediction that nothing could prevent his own doom and that of his race, the king appeared on the rooftop in an attempt to placate his subjects. He was struck by a stray stone that inflicted a slight wound on his brow, and from this he died, having lost all will to live.

All hell was now let loose. The Spaniards, loading themselves with treasure, tried to withdraw under cover of night, but a frenzied onslaught from the Aztecs resulted in the slaughter of half of Cortes's force and the loss of all the guns and horses, not to mention the booty. As he retreated northward, columns of smoke and agonized screams rose from the apex of the temples where the priests were busily disposing of such fallen Spaniards as still had life in them.

Cortes established himself at a base about a hundred miles away, from which, a year later, with a following of Indian warriors commanded by Spaniards, he forced his way back into Tenochtitlan. The battle, against overwhelming odds, raged night and day for seventy-five days. If the Aztecs had been content to kill their enemies rather than to capture them alive as food for their gods, they could not have failed to win. Eventually, however, Montezuma's successor, Cuahtemoc, fell into Spanish hands, and the Aztec nation suddenly collapsed. The population left the city in a body, flowing soundlessly across the causeways for three days and nights, leaving fifty thousand dead behind them. Their golden city had been reduced to rubble.

Cortes at once began to build a New Jerusalem upon the ruins of the old walls, including a magnificent palace for himself on the site of Montezuma's. But his success and wealth aroused bitter jealousy among his rivals, and the king of Spain presently appointed a viceroy over him. Although ennobled, worshipped as a god by the Indians, and the possessor of vast estates, Cortes was left without authority and soon his achievement was eclipsed by that of Pizarro and his conquest of Peru.

On returning to the Spanish court in 1547, Cortes was ignored by his capricious sovereign. On his way back to Mexico the conqueror was struck down with a fever from which he died at the age of sixty-two.

About thirty miles away, at the culmination of the somber Avenue of the Dead, stand the ruins of the Toltec city of Teotihuacan. A labyrinth of monasteries and temples, it was once the earthly abode of the all-powerful god Quetzalcoatl,

A labyrinth of monasteries and temples, it was once the earthly abode of the all-powerful god Quetzacoatl. Teotihuacan, Mexico. Photograph by Francisco Uribe.

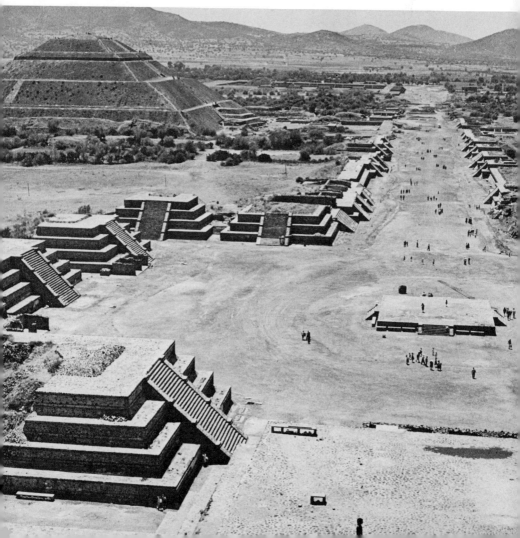

whose vengeful return to annihilate the Aztecs was believed to be incarnated in the person of Cortes. Quetzalcoatl, one of the few gods who was opposed to human sacrifice, was believed, like Aphrodite of ancient Greece, to have emerged at birth fully mature from a gastropod shell. Indeed the walls of his palace shimmered with mother-of-pearl, and the frieze around his innermost sanctuary consisted of a closely observed design of pecten shells. The various thrones from which he presided were invariably formed from a single shell, and many of the sacred tombs disclosed one perfect univalve lying beside the solitary occupant. Perhaps the simple beauty of the shell was intended to bring solace to the entombed spirit, for through the ages in religious symbolism it has signified purity, forgiveness, redemption, and resurrection.

Teotihuacan, illumined from afar by the overlasting snows of Popocatepetl and of Ixtaccihuatl, the "smoking mountain" and the "white lady," is at the time of our visit the background for a season of *son et lumière*. The city is dominated by two pyramids—one dedicated to the sun god, the other to the moon. From each prodigious pile in turn a flood of proudly spoken words pours through the loudspeakers and thins out into the encircling hills. We are listening to pronouncements of the gods taken from the inscriptions on the walls of the sanctuaries. The powerful impact of these words, the rolling of huge snake-skin drums, and the pillars of smoke rising from the zenith of each shrine set the imagination working upon the bloody rites committed at their summits. The Azecs believed that the sun god was kept alive by human sacrifices, without which it would literally fall from the sky and the world be plunged into perpetual darkness. In full view of the populace, therefore, each victim was forced to ascend a steep flight of steps to the sacrificial stone at the apex. Here he was stripped and pinned down by four priests. The presiding priest then plunged a knife into his breast, thrust in a hand and drew forth the heart, which he would toss into the belly of the god. The priests saturated their robes and their hair with blood, while dark crimson rivers of it overflowed from the platform and ran down the walls. When the sun was at a certain angle the king himself would act as high priest, and the slaughter

50

would endure for days on end, with the death roll amounting to over fifty thousand. Bodies were flung from the eminence, and the limbs hacked off so that the spectators might enjoy a sacrificial dinner.

The gruesome scenes impelled the Spaniards to annihilate the priesthood, the sanctuaries, and, above all, the gods themselves. As a matter of fact, the Aztec civilization, as well as those preceding it, was in many respects infinitely superior to the one existing in Spain at the time of the conquest. In the destruction of the outrageous Aztec gods, much was lost that was altogether enlightened and noble.

It is impossible not to be profoundly moved by the poverty here, which washes to the very walls of all the cities in a filthy tide of hovels swarming with apathetic children, adults, old crones, pye-dogs, pigs, poultry, and rats. As we pass through these wretched shanty towns I turn cold with shock, anger, and a deep sadness. To dwell further on this misery and degradation would be to write a different sort of book, but it is a constant dark presence in the experience of Mexico and one that lingers in the mind long after the brilliant colors have faded.

3 Fiji

Mindful of the vein of insecurity that ran through our recent expedition to Mexico, caused by living throughout like two birds on a bough, we have had arrangements for a trip to Fiji buttoned up for months in advance. Pillows on which to lay our heads and plane seats between one pillow and the next are firmly booked and confirmed. At Fiji, a fisherman and his boat await us on the shore and a Mr. Walai has been engaged to guide us to the shelling reefs; berths have been reserved on a coaster trading between Lautoka and the Outer Isles, and an interview has been arranged with the Right Honorable Ratu Sir Kamisese Mara, overlord of Lau and knight of the British Empire. What prospect could look blander?

Nevertheless, a cloud considerably larger than a man's hand becomes visible around noon when a car appears to take us to Heathrow. The driver arrives so early that I fob him off to the pub, and as he casts off from one end of Onslow Square, Pat erupts at the other.

"Get weaving!" Pat cries crisply. "Pan Am's gone on strike! We'll just make the last plane if we hurry. Where's the car? I told the bloke to come half an hour earlier."

O miserere! Where indeed? We bid an absentminded farewell to our staff, both of whom are also on strike, and transfer four leaden suitcases to the curb edge. The airport naturally is in chaos, and against this disheveled background we re-visualize the next few weeks. What about going to Fiji the other way round the world? Or to Australia, perhaps, or to Hong

Kong? These deliberations are interrupted by an announcement in Middle Western and in Spanish that our flight is about to take off via the polar route.

Malossol caviar is washed down by vodka and succeeded by steak from the perfumed pastures of Texas with champagne and some frozen Brie. During this meal a talkie is shown in silence, its sound track having apparently joined the strike. Presently the plane turns deathly cold and I retire to the rest room to draw on some woollen tights, whilst most of the customers disappear under blankets. A casual glance downward reveals what is unmistakably the moon. There it is, the pitch terrain overpitted with craters now as familiar to us as S.W.7. (Thy will be done, on earth and on the moon, as it is in Heaven.) When we eventually flop into Los Angeles it is through the usual stinging smog. By now the strike has struck in earnest. An ulcer-provoking confrontation takes place in the sanctum of the airport between the strikers and the only surviving Pan Am executive, who tries but fails to reroute us onward.

Towards evening he succeeds. We take a hop into San Francisco to join a BOAC jet, which is bound for Fiji and off schedule through having had to deliver spare parts to a sister plane marooned in a stage of collapse on the tarmac. Off we go. On comes the caviar and champagne, Californian this time. Eleven hours after leaving San Francisco, having crossed the dateline and mislaid Sunday altogether, an emblazoned sky, brassy as a *Murex brassica*, heralds the break of whatever day it now is, and we emerge gratefully into the dulcet air of the Fijian island of Viti Levu. *O ni sa yadra!* Good morning, good morning! The airport receptionist and money changer is the Princess Adi Samanunu Qalirea Cakebau, known as Sammy, a great-granddaughter of the last cannibal chief, Saru Cakebau, reputed at a conservative estimate to have eaten one thousand persons.

Conical hills lie about us, capped with patches of emerald sugarcane and golden corn, studded with mango and casuarina trees and threaded with crystalline streams. Brilliantly clean children, in starched white cotton and with lustrous black hair, are streaming blithely off to school. By the time we arrive at the Korolevu Hotel seventy miles along the coral coast, we are in no fit state to consume the third breakfast of the last eight hours; but we eat it, nevertheless, before passing out in the somewhat sketchy quarters assigned to us. Our closing eyes rest upon palm trees writhing in a squall, while in our ears echo the bucketing of rain and the bellowing of surf upon the reef.

Twenty chains away (about a quarter of a mile) in an open-sided hut overhanging the bay, Jahaw the carver sits cross-legged on the ground, surrounded by his apprentices. With primitive tools they are fashioning masks, figures, and animals from fine-grained wood. Also a forest of totem poles. "Phallic symbols," pronounces Pat, a gleam in his eye. ("What's so special about a phallic symbol anyway?," Jung once inquired, "It's only a male organ.") A wave of hilarity ripples through the hut as, admirably at ease, the occupants struggle ardently and politely to express themselves in English. We emerge the owners of a mask carved from rosewood and sorrowful as a Pièta, and of an implacable male head crowned with hibiscus, knowing well that neither is suitable for Onslow Square or anywhere else we are likely to live.

On a track running down to the shore, ravishing young cowboys rip past us bareback on apricot-hued ponies with streaming manes and tails and tagged close in to heel by wild-looking lurchers. Their easy mastery over their cattle —Brahmins with upturned curvaceous horns—is impressive. The track peters out onto a beach smothered in ocean rubble, twiglets of coral, flinty stones, and piles of shells, all encrusted with limelike whitened calcium. We gather a school of auger shells, several jasper-hued turbans with opercula-like glass eyes, and a bouquet of rose pearl tops, only momentarily deterred by the knowledge of what such calcareous encrustation involves. The outlook is one of burned fingers, inflamed eyes, and drops of caustic soda on the linoleum eating its way into the promises below.

A coconut stabbed through the heart by a long dagger lies under a palm tree, like the Theomanic stone impaled by Excalibur. With somewhat unregal exertion I succeed in extracting it, wondering if I may not thereby be destined for the Fijian crown? At the first flash of the blade, however, a radiant boy shoots out of the undergrowth. Light seems to shake out of his hair and to radiate from his torso. His indigo eyes, which gaze straight into mine, are centered with blazing black pupils. This is our first exposure to the formidable Fijian charm, and we get the full treatment. With a respectful bow he claims the knife as his own and introduces himself as Sabu. Then, taking a wildcat run up the trunk of a towering palm tree, he slashes at some coconuts, which hurtle alarmingly earthward. Sitting in the shade, we share the milk and the sweet white flesh of the fruit, which he exposes with a few furious swipes of his machete. His thirst for information seems unquenchable. Under an onslaught of pointed questions relating to Pat's calling, his gold reserves, and our prowess in begetting—the Fijians love the "begats"—we find ourselves being gradually impelled towards his village, Vatua. It lies in a gardenlike compound that encircles a sheltered creek. Sabu's family *bure,* or hut, is heavily thatched, and in each of the walls, formed of bamboo canes interlaced with palm, a wide entrance is set in lieu of windows.

Layers of matting cover the floor so that the family can be, and as a matter of fact is, sleeping comfortably everywhere. Sabu's mother squats within a crescent of cooking pots that simmer merrily on a log fire. She sniffs each in turn. Yams; beans; fish chowder; a sort of stew. It smells delectable. Ringed around with Sabu's brothers, we sink to the floor together to examine his treasures—polished coconut beans, shell leis, turtleshell, a *Mitra taeniata* (a perfect spiral in orange, black and white), a map cowry, and a cone that we take to be the common lettered variety but that later reveals two additional rows of brown spots, turning it into a collector's item, the *Conus capitaneus.* We offer Sabu a little more than the modest price he is asking, and, with perfectly timed reluctance, he accepts. As we take a ceremonious leave, however, with a lordly gesture he makes us a present of the lot.

The wind is squalling and the reef booming on our side of the headland when we return. Pat has hired a fishing boat for the afternoon, and it awaits him in a cove, rearing and plunging like a mustang. He and its grinning skipper take off lightly and easily into the boiling surf. They reappear three hours later, soaked to the skin, without having been able to exchange a word nor make a single strike, yet both are oddly fulfilled and at ease.

The Fijian Islands were accidentally discovered in the mid-seventeenth century by navigators on their way elsewhere. What they saw here discouraged them from doing more than merely registering their existence. Captains Cook and Bligh came in 1774 and 1789 respectively. At this time the ten thousand or so islands were divided into about six kingdoms, varying in size and power according to the ability and energy of the current chief, or ratu. It was all very unsettling and exhausting, and by 1874 a chief already mentioned, Cakebau, with some of his fellow rulers, were thankful to hand over the lot to Britain in an act of cession.

The capital was shifted from Levuka to Suva to be at the hub, and, from that day until October 10, 1970, the whole affair went with a swing. Now power has been invested once more in the Fijians, with results yet to be seen. For the moment these are still celestial islands, which seem to breed some special grace, a matchless gentleness, ease, and gaiety. Fiji brims with those who came here once on holiday and have stayed ever since. We even contemplate following their example.

In Fiji if you ask a negative question it will almost certainly be answered in the affirmative. Those are, par excellence, "yes" people. It was in a Suva market that an Australian once asked: "You haven't got any bananas, have you?" and got the answer immortalized in song: "Yes, we have no bananas." The Fijians are sable-dark in complexion, with wide shoulders tapering into narrow waists. Their columnlike necks support a square head held high, haloed with fuzzy black hair. Their eyes blaze with benevolence, and their serene features radiate sympathy and forebearance. The male wears a sort of wrapped skirt, the sulu, much as the Scots wear a kilt. All are swathed in gaudy cotton, brilliant as parakeets, beflowered at the neck and hair. Nearly all the Indian population have taken to European dress, although the fine-boned women sometimes float past in their pastel saris, delicate as a bunch of sweet peas. The Chinese, predominantly merchants and shopkeepers, are concentrated in the large towns where trade flourishes. Identical little shops selling identical goods are brooded over by indistinguishable Celestials in washed-out blue cotton. It is a mystery how they prosper, if indeed they do. Public notices are therefore printed in four tongues, Fijian, Indian, and Chinese, with the addition of English.

The evening brings a Fijian entertainment, which is performed almost out of sight on the far side of the swimming pool. Although a drought is supposed to be ruining the crops, it drizzles throughout, but the dancing and a barbecue progress guilelessly, if moistly. An examination of the buffet raises a gastronomic problem. Octopus salad; sockeye salmon curry (tinned, with unidentified additions); stuffed (with what?) pumpkin; Chinese ham and clams on fried rice; local drink on the house from a bamboo cup. Since we are eating by what would be moonlight if it did not happen to be raining, it is difficult to identify the unfamiliar flavors, and we might be, and indeed are, eating almost anything.

Meanwhile, gorgeous girls wearing anklets of leaves and crowned in flowers are swaying together like ripe wheat in the breeze, gesturing mysteriously in the manner of temple dancers. Their men accompany them by pounding on the grass with hollow bamboo poles of varying girth, and with a harmony of song so close that it might be one despairing voice crying for the moon. Soon all the guests themselves are dancing, kicking off their shoes, threading blossoms through their hair and borrowing leis of flowers. Ah, Polynesia!—Or are we perhaps in Melanesia? An air of trans-Pacific chic pervades the party, which is mainly from Australia, forthright, energetic, and equipped with particularly fine lungs. When, therefore, we retire in the early hours from Bedlam into bed it is not, alas, to sleep.

The news travels round the dining room that there is to be a wedding at the local church and that all are bidden. Brimming with bonhomie, guests from the hotel troop into the village just as the bride appears, submerged in a pea green

Mother Hubbard, sans flowers, sans bridesmaids, sans anything, and thrumming like a smitten harp with suppressed sobs. We first assume this afflicted figure to be her mother. A few subdued guests presently slink into the church, where much murmuring and bowing occurs before a Chinese priest. Who is marrying whom? No one can make it out. Later, Asunta, our waitress, divulges that the bride is "in foal" and that her father has declared that unless the couple marry he will slit their throats. We slip away from this joyless occasion to wander home through fields like flower gardens, where the path winds between twin pools from which violet, white, and shocking pink water lilies thrust upward on long stalks, looking like hallucinatory daisies.

The splendid Mr. Walai, our guide, awaits us in the hall on our return, a towering Fijian of formidable proportions and of total charm. A warm regard radiates from under a peaceful brow, while his manner is one of leisurely courtesy. He has laid on a car to drive us to the island of Serua some sixteen hundred chains, or twenty miles, away. The tide is out and the causeway ankle-deep in water, so we set off to wade across the channel to the beach opposite. Presently the water deepens and the sand begins to teem with menacing shapes—long leopardine snakes, globoid sea slugs, the writhing centipede arms of spider starfish, bloated black serpents, sea urchins with quills like hatpins, and a myriad of mud-clogged shapes that creep, roll, and burrow on the bottom. The scene is also bespeckled with a thriving crop of crown of thorns, a species of starfish whose sting takes eight months to heal. Thank Heaven for sneakers, a stout stick, and gardening gloves. Even so, it is a testing experience to close the hand upon some slime-ridden creature who, although endowed with admirable qualities and no doubt kind to his mother, lacks personal magnetism. It may, for instance, possess five tentacles, one of which contains a stomach bag, the next an eye, the third a feeler, another a foot, while the fifth terminates in a sting.

"No good being squeamish," says Pat hardily, scenting disenchantment. To demonstrate his unconcern he loops up a

Mr. Walai, our guide of formidable proportions and total charm, with his wife outside his house in Vatua, Fiji. Photograph by Patrick Hodgson.

three-foot sea snake on his stick. It flashes round like a whip, fixing teeth like needles into his glove, which he throws off with a yell.

"It won't hurt you," soothes Walai in the even tones of the hotel receptionist recommending a bath in the shark pool—meaning, I presume, it probably won't kill you. Nevertheless, Pat is subsequently bitten on the shin by one of these reptiles and bears the scar to this hour.

We set out to wade across the channel to Serua Island. Walai and Martha Hodgson. Photograph by Patrick Hodgson.

On glancing up from a patch of shells through which I am sifting, I am disconcerted to find that both men have disappeared. A sense of absolute isolation awakens within me a sharp awareness of the teeming primeval life unlocked around me, and with it a powerful curiosity not untinged with fear. A transparent green crab with pinpoint periscope eyes pauses in its skittering run. We exchange a speculative glance before he sidles under cover. Pink caterpillars, covered with black bristles like overblown bladders, lie motionless in serpentine curves. Huge starfish sprawl marooned in the shallows awaiting the turn of the tide. The landscape looks exaggerated and illusory. "All is calm," I sing shakily to the empty sky, assailed by a sensation of unreality, "All is bright . . ."

60

"Shut up!" expostulates Pat, rising from behind a boulder where he has been deliberating over a deep pool full of aquatic characters intent upon their private errands. Joining him on the verge we catch glimpses of trails of shivering seaweed vibrating with hidden life. Fronds of sea anemones unfold and close again upon their invisible prey; bleeding teeth nerites cleave to rocks, exposing an impenetrable operculum when we prize them off. Presently, we see the trail of a living shell, a four-inch virgin cone, which when eventually scraped clean is a tender pink, terminating in a violet flush. It is respectfully garnered at its widest point, as cones should be, since many harbor a poisoned barb, the sting from which has often proved fatal. Dead shells, often tenanted by hermit crabs, bright and brittle as dried flowers, lie in drifts upon the shore. After disentangling several yards of living matter from a seven-pronged shape, a scorpion conch emerges; this, despite its aggressive outline, is an amiable vegetarian that lays its eggs in masses of innocuous spaghetti. On overturning a rock I pounce on a tiger cowry, sleek as satin, dappled with black and tan flecks. At the initial touch its membrane frill folds up and disappears into the cavity between its glittering teeth. The fascination deepens. Impervious to time and tide, to the burning sun, a rasping wind, to reddening eyes, and to backache, we potter intently onward, each of us absorbed in our private adventure.

When Walai hails us from afar, blowing upon a triton shell, we naturally ignore so aggravating an interruption. In the end, however, the message penetrates: if we do not cross now, we will spend the night here.

The channel has broadened and the tide is whirling like Charybdis. Shuddering at the memory of the rocky pools and of their uncongenial occupants, I murmur, but without much hope, that perhaps we could get a boat; one lies drawn up on the shore.

"No, no. We walk," says Walai firmly. "Follow me." In the master's steps we tread, more or less, with water foaming to our thighs, unmentionable matter swirling round our ankles, the shore as remote as the Garden of Eden and at least as desirable. It is a long crunch, not without incident, but finally we make it.

Meanwhile, we have communicated to Walai our determination, should we reach dry land unscathed, to find a golden cowry for our collection in London. Twice recently we have been outbid at Sotheby's for a specimen that would rate as dross in Serua. The south shore of Viti Levu, which we are approaching, is known to yield one occasionally, and Walai thinks that in the neighboring hamlet of Komaye a fisherman's wife has made a recent find. We draw up presently near this village to be instantly encircled by the usual formula of hilarious adults, skipping children, dogs, cats, sepia pigs, and a donkey or two. A gay procession through the compound ends in a *bure* where, cross-legged on the floor under a portrait of the Queen, sits a monolithic bronze lady, her golden cowry at the ready, swathed in a roll of magenta silk, packed with desiccated coconut to add luster and reduce odor. The cowry is a warm shade of apricot, fluent in outline and elegantly etched with ivory, but it lacks, alas, the burnish of the shell found alive. All the same we cannot resist it, poor thing, and after some dignified bartering, Pat buys it to give it a home. I slip it under my pillow when I go to bed, where its pale presence penetrates a waking hour in which stealthy movements on the linoleum announce that a hermit crab, the lessee of a phos whelk, has flung himself off the dressing table and, shell on back, is stumping sturdily home to the sea.

Suva, the capital city, is an eighty-mile flight away over the mountains, but on the morning that Pat has resolved to discharge certain duties there the daily plane develops some aeronautical hitch, surprise, surprise. The minister for tourism opportunely provides him with a lift in his car and they disappear together in a cloud of dust.

The reception desk is deserted by all but David, an envoy with a scrolled moustache, whose fuzzy hair forms a halo a foot wide around his head. Communication between us seems blocked, Fijian charm for some reason being turned off at the main. I am perplexed by the thunderous ambience. What has gone amiss? Can the stench of decaying fish that I have been assuming to originate in the kitchen actually be emanating from me? From, let's face it, a pocket in my sarong? Investigation reveals two cowries, earmarked for burial under a night-blooming cereus and there to be consumed by ants, decomposing disgracefully upon my person. I feel quite mortified for them. Why not, I reflect, experiment instead with the coral sand and seawater method? Accordingly, I crouch at the ocean verge agitating the cowries abrasively, first in one then in the other. How successful this would have proved I am unable to report, for without warning a wave double the size of any preceding it engulfs me, the cowries, my dark glasses, and the selected poems of John Betjeman, and together we all disappear into the surf. This predicament seems to strike some familiar chord:

"I have been here before, where or when I cannot tell."

The answer to the riddle comes down the wind of which, as usual, there is plenty. This ocean, remember, is the so-called Pacific.

Headlines in the *Fiji Times* this morning report that a postman in Suva has just been awarded the Albert medal for driving off a shark which had bitten off his fiancée's foot. I draw Walai's attention to this. His sole comment is that sharks never bite off human feet unless they are hungry, but better not wear anything in the sea that gleams. I banish a ring from my finger and the polish from my finger and toenails and plunge into the ocean. No living soul is in sight, all other bathers seeming to prefer the pool for, I suspect, some very good reason. However, with feet intact I am returning to anchorage when Walai rounds the bend in a state of high excitement. He looks behind him conspiritorially and hisses (or would have hissed if there had been sibilants in the words Golden cowry). "Golden cowry! Follow me."

Together we skirt the fire walkers' pit and approach a delegation drawn up behind the laundry. The central figure, the dead spit of the late Queen Salote, is clad in hot pink and sits broodingly upon the grass with several children heaped up on her lap. A guardian brother, in army surplus khaki, closely attends her, plus several outlying sisters. From a length of silk she slowly unwraps a stunning golden cowry, brilliant as a gem, pure in outline, of a radiant luster and texture. I am as one who first looks into Chapman's Homer. Walai conducts the negotiation in Fijian, to which, with the shell glowing in my hand and my heart and my mind already made up, I pay but perfunctory attention. An astronomical sum is named, at which I automatically demur . . . but, after some further exchange she agrees to take sixty pounds in sterling. I rush into the hotel to change more traveler's checks. The party from Vatukarasa, where the cowry was found on the reef four months ago, is in a gala mood when I return, all anxiety having fled. To the Fijian, the find of a golden cowry is the equivalent of winning the Irish Sweep, but their problem is to bypass the middleman who deprives them of most of the profit.

The evening gives rise to a dance in the laundry for the hotel staff, heavily patronized also by the guests. The Fijian girls are demurely clad in mission-house mother hubbards, their men in somber European dress. When we arrive they are dancing chastely together as if in the Methodist church hall. Several Australian girls in immoderate minis, however, pick out partners from among the male staff with whom they whirl like dervishes, making frenzied gestures of unequivocal invitation. One of these is a twenty-year-old bride on her honeymoon, so she probably does not mean what her gestures imply, but is this understood by the porter with whom she is now dancing?

The triweekly barbecue and entertainment that occurs in the garden is beginning to take its toll on long-term customers. Once monthly, however, the routine is broken by the enactment of the Yaqona ceremony of welcome. Pat is invited to be the honored guest by Bill Clark, the hotel owner who, in a scarlet Fijian sulu with a white lei and a hibiscus tucked behind his ear, is a particularly striking figure tonight with his Viking blue eyes and golden white hair.

The intention is that the scene shall be lit by moonlight, but the moon has once more taken the evening off. Flanked by two befeathered Fijians, Pat is led forward and solemnly enthroned. Laid at his feet is a twist of rope, interspersed with glossy white egg cowries which here symbolize honor and precedence. Drawn up in the darkness stand a phalanx of

The Yaqona ceremony of welcome, at which Pat is invited to be the honored guest. Photograph by Rob Wright, Jr., Fiji Visitors Bureau.

warriors headed by a chieftain, all in full paraphernalia of grass skirts, feathers, beads, shells, flowers, and war paint, their hair powdered with kura root. Like an armorial trophy they prickle from all angles with spears, knives, axes, and shields. Floodlights blaze on, dramatically illuminating a tableau that might be cast in bronze. There is a lengthy unblinking silence. At last the chieftain begins to chant, arms outflung heavenward. With bowed heads the warriors respond. Drums roll. Bamboo poles thud. An immense wooden bowl is set before the chieftain, into which liquid from a six-foot bamboo vessel is ceremoniously poured. *Vau*, the root of a fibrous creeper, is immersed in this fluid, in which the chief laves his hands and arms, periodically wringing out the vine into the bowl. This ritual is repeated seven times.

65

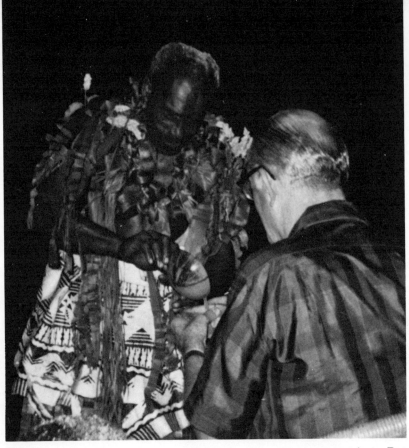

Dipping a coconut shell into the liquid, a warrior presents it to Pat with profound obeisance. Yaqona ceremony of welcome. Photograph by Martha Hodgson.

A warrior then approaches and, dipping a coconut shell into the liquid, presents it to Pat with a profound obeisance. Pat, although the possessor of a hypersensitive palate, does not flinch. He is required to strike his hands together, lift the cup aloft, and drain it to the dregs (of which there are plenty); and, to his eternal credit, he does it. A ferocious yell announces that the welcome is now accomplished. The warriors instantly become involved in a furious war dance. They stamp towards us with diabolical howls, distorted features, and leveled spears, each to his chosen victim. Eye to eye, breast to breast, glaring virulently, they pause, immobile. I am nonplussed to recognize the ebony nose within an inch of my own as that of Josef, our particularly obliging waiter, now looking as if he would gladly dish me up as stew. Maybe this is about to occur. Let me think

. . . how long ago is it, do you suppose, since the last cannibal retired? Haven't I read recently a comforting report that Fijians have always preferred to dine off one another, "white long pig" being both stringy and too saline for the Fijian palate?

Mark Twain once remarked, "If you don't like our weather, wait a minute."

We have waited philosophically and now a golden morning is here, windless, the air heavy with the scent of summer and the boom of bees speeding from one magnolia to the next. In this appetite-provoking ambience it becomes urgent to introduce a reform of the daily menu. From this morning onward we sustain life mainly at breakfast. Not even Fijian cooking can blight canned orange juice, cornflakes, poached eggs, honey, instant coffee, and fresh pineapple, nor a luncheon consisting of a cheese sandwich. Plenty can happen, and does, at the nightly repast, but when necessary we can survive until morning on a roll, butter, and a bottle of beer. The alternative is to migrate to the newly opened Hotel Fijian. Bent upon investigating this possibility, we bump westward over some twenty circuitous and dusty miles, taking in the small town of Sigitoka, where the shops and their contents exude the very essence of India. We fall, with hardly a struggle, for some jazzed up Goanese shirts that far outfish Mr. Fish, a black pearl, a cerise sari, white jasmine incense, and a sack of succulent mandarins. The route is edged with trudging figures, to many of whom we give a lift. Each displays the all-pervading loving kindness of the Fijian in whatever form of communication he has at his disposal. The children speak English and can thus find expression for their goodwill, but their elders have recourse only to nods and becks and wreathèd smiles. One appreciative passenger flings a thank offering of a rock-hard passion fruit through the window, nearly putting out Pat's eye.

We find the Hotel Fijian to be splendidly sited on the island of Yanuca, joined to the mainland by a causeway, and crowning a sheltered horseshoe bay. Its architecture combines the Fijian with the international in a manner described as "totally now!" Here, although the patrons look a shade ritzier than ours, the cuisine strikes an identical note. Reconciled, therefore, to our domestic arrangements, we are heading towards home when our attention is drawn to a reef, close inshore and dankly emerging with the falling tide. In five minutes, efficiently equipped and going evenly, Pat is crunching off across the coral towards the horizon.

"No good being squeamish," I remark to a passing parakeet, and take off in pursuit. Stepping absentmindedly in a hole, I fall flat on my face into a pool writhing with loathsome shapes. My stick floats past en route to the open sea.

At each high tide a glass-bottomed boat takes off for the reef, from which the customers can brood over the fabulously hued schools of fish that dart in between banks of majestic elkhead coral and forests of purple and citrine sea fans, intricate as snow flakes. Ribbons of seaweed sway between ridges of multicolored coral. As the water deepens, we discern a shark skulking on the seabed, the darting head of a moray eel, the undulating arms of an octopus, and a gleaming egg cowry with its pleated black mantle fully extended. I recall a childhood hero of mine, the keeper of the lock of Chertsey-on-Thames: "The ocean beds would be in full flower now," he once remarked dreamily. "It's lovelier there than my rose garden is in full bloom." He had been a deep-sea diver somewhere in the Pacific, as well as with Shackleton on his last polar expedition, and was finding the Chertsey Meads a bit flat.

Walai is awaiting our return in the shallows and wades out to pull the boat. Grasping Pat by the arm, he murmurs urgently into his ear while they fade off together into a grove of fern trees.

I stretch out on the hot sand under a palm, reconciled to God and man, drowsily contemplating the curvaceous waving of the fronds. Whang! A coconut plummets down like a bomb, almost burying itself with the force of its descent. I do not stir. What better way to perish than by being instantaneously brained by a coconut at the moment when I have become aware of the inmost meaning of life, even if for the moment I cannot remember exactly what it is?

Pat and Walai reappear, immensely animated, in the company of a circular Fijian presence, brilliantly clad and permanently convulsed with mirth. He introduces himself as the ratu mara of Serua Island, where he invites us tomorrow to a fish-spearing party, ha, ha, ha! Will we feast with him in the Vale Vakaturaga, ha, ha, and meet his wife and fruit—er—family? Pat and Walai, obviously heavy with tidings, politely brush off the ratu by loading him into a yellow taxi in which he is borne from sight still laughing uproariously and full of hospitable plans for the morrow. With a well-timed gesture, Pat produces a golden cowry like a topaz pear from under his shirt. It is at least an inch longer than any other we have yet experienced. Walai and Pat have been bartering in the fern grove with an aunt of Walai's who, having heard by bush telegraph methods that serious buyers are at Korolevu, has trudged from her village two thousand chains hence, her treasure in her petticoat pocket.

Walai is radiant at his success, so we take him to our bed-room to inspect the entire hoard. The golden cowry is estab-lished upon a low table and we gather round it, silenced by its

A golden cowry from Viti Levu, Fiji. (*Cypraea aurantium* Gmelin). Photograph by Sara Heaton.

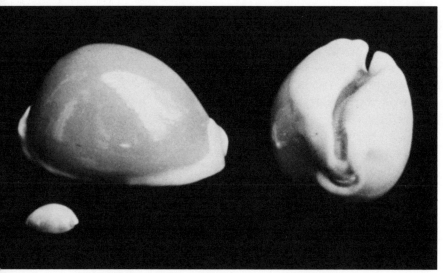

pure perfection. In Japan, I have read, collectors meet in sessions known as "Inspiration," when they sit in prolonged contemplation of a single shell at a time. If they feel inspired to give vent to their emotion about any particular specimen, they compare it to some known object—to a hand, a flower, a cloud, a fan, or a bird. We have pondered upon what reward can be offered to a man like Walai, who has already inherited the earth. Money seems inappropriate, although a modest sum has already changed hands and been absently but gracefully received. So what else? In our luggage is a Wedgewood tankard commemorating the Prince of Wales's investiture, intended by us for Ratu Sir Kamisese Mara, which we now bestow upon Walai. He receives it with gentle dignity. "My wife and I will keep it forever," he says, his eyes misting over, "and our children after us." This is almost too much for us. Stiffening the upper lip we clatter hastily off, laden with the usual paraphernalia, to explore some remote reef recommended by Walai.

This reef has a few new pitfalls up its sleeve. It consists of miles of flat wastes of coral covered uniformly with six inches of water. Canyons intersect the desolation into which prudence suggests I do not venture. I wait, therefore, until Pat and Walai have crunched off, the crust periodically collapsing under their weight, and then take a cool-eyed reconnaissance. Sea slugs lie in heaps, looking as if they had been blown up with bicycle pumps. Crowns of thorns are burgeoning everywhere, like a rock garden. The reef is pockmarked with barnacles and ridged over with spines of ashen coral, cuts from which invariably go septic. What a prospect! What a shambles! My thoughts turn, and not for the last time, towards the gleaming shores of Marco, Sanibel, and the Cayman Islands, where shells lie waiting to be garnered like flowers upon the silver sand. This nostalgic train of thought is shattered by the eruption upon the landscape of what, at a cursory glance, appears to be an outsize frog. A preliminary croak divulges this plodding figure to be one of the fishing fraternity from the Korelevu, now in the role of skindiver and photographer. We muse together on the hazards of malacology, about which he takes a pessimistic view.

The ratu mara of Serua Island and his wife, Princess Adi Tufoa.
Photograph by Patrick Hodgson.

"You must be very, vary careful," he warns. "Your shoes
are much too thin for the many, many sea urchins underfoot,
not to mention the knife edges of coral reef. And then your
gloves! Any bristle worm could sting through those, and the
pools are full of 'em. So take care where you put your hands!
Besides, this reef positively stinks with moray eels, and once

their jaws lock, they're locked for good!" On this blithe note he webfoots off into the ocean, whose waters receive him with a sigh. I retreat to the shore, sink easefully down upon a rock under a palm and produce my recorder. The reedy notes of "O for the Wings of a Dove" and "You Can't Get a Man with a Gun" intrigue the mynah birds, which have a go in turn, somewhat off key.

The morning of the ratu's party on Serua to watch the spear fishing is mercifully clement. A swarm of guests traverses the channel in flat-bottomed punts (no nonsense about wading this time), each poled pliantly from the stern by one of our hosts. An uproarious greeting from the ratu awaits us on the dock, which bends precariously under his three hundred pounds. With a munificent gesture, he throws open his tiny kingdom for us to wander in at will until luncheon in the *vale,* or chiefly house.

Serua, we find, is simply Viti Levu in miniature. It seems it is the solemn duty of the ruler to cultivate a spectacular girth. When he presides at the seat of justice he should resemble a well-based pyramid and, should he lose weight, he will include porpoise in his diet to restore it. His subjects are to be seen pottering innocently in their compounds, occasionally net-mending, cooking, pounding, potting, or plaiting palm leaves. Orderly peach-colored children emerge, grin engagingly, but maintain reserve. This morning a baby has been born in a shack built over the water on stilts. The laughing mother, the baby like a fresh bun at her breast, points to him proudly as we pass. The solitary hill is crowned by a house owned by the ratu's brother, complete with linoleum, a piano, and a framed letter from the Queen in the parlor.

Luncheon starts with soup made by boiling seashells (many of them specimens coveted by us) and simply pouring off the broth into coconut shells. Waha, a local fish, follows, steamed in coconut milk, embedded on fragrant leaves and served with boiled seaweed, mashed coconut, yams, palm hearts, and corn on the cob. Pumpkin Russe completes the menu. The ratu then emits a series of unnerving backfires, after which he and his guests together sink to the floor of the chiefly house for a siesta, lying flat on several layers of matting.

Orderly children grin engagingly but maintain reserve. Fiji. Photograph by Patrick Hodgson.

A fleet of punts is lurching violently in the channel, for the tide is now running in one direction with the wind blowing in the other. The guests are distributed among the craft. As each boat clears the shelter of a spit of land it is met by a smack from the elements that soaks the occupants to the skin. On the horizon an assembly of boats can be seen converging upon some shallows. It is a cold, sick ride. We find the entire shoal encompassed within a vast garland that is woven from strands of ropy vine and interwoven with palms. The fishermen are beginning to shorten it as we approach, encircling the fish in an ever-decreasing space. The guests, who are all drenched anyway, join their hosts already waist-deep in water. Together they haul in the vine, which progressively thickens the walls

73

of the trap. The enclosed fish begin to leap and thresh frantically. The spearmen steady themselves with poised shafts for the attack. The ring grows progressively smaller. Two enormous fish fling themselves at the obstacle and, after a frenzied struggle, escape through it amid a storm of yells and oaths. Smaller fish take advantage of the diversion to whip through the tangle of limbs, vines, and leaves, into which obviously no fisherman can thrust a spear. Order is restored at last. The remaining fish are left agitatedly nosing the walls of the trap. Chanting ceremoniously, the prime fisherman scatters some powder in amongst them. The effect is electric. The fish go berserk; they change color; they leap, flap, and turn turtle. One by one they are impaled on Neptune-like tridents and with whoops of triumph are borne shoreward in great reed baskets to be barbecued later on the beach. Their exquisite sheen and sumptuous color fades into a mournful grey as they are conveyed from the scene. Later, we learn that the use of this poison is illegal. It is obtained from the hulu or barringtonia tree, a spectacular magnolia bearing heavily perfumed flowers the size of soup plates, the seeds of which contain the perfidious venom.

By the time we get home, the hairdresser is shut. A mixture of sand, salt, and dust, with the addition of some eight-hour cream recommended to me by Elizabeth Arden, who used it on her racehorses, has produced a sculptured effect. I look, in profile, somewhat like the knave of spades. The hotel boutique is operated by Jean Scott—before the week is out she is to become the Fijian beauty queen—who, producing the key to the barbershop, volunteers to give me a shampoo. She pours a mixture over my coiffure that immediately turns solid. For instant beauty just add water. Taxed to the limit of her ingenuity, it takes Jean two hours to render me down. As a thank offering for her exertions I give her some French earrings that she has admired. She sends a rare spindle shell up to my room. I write a note of thanks. Dinnertime brings an answer and a rose. The ball is now in my court, but I concede her game, set, and match.

Recently a golden cowry reached a high price at Sotheby's because it was suggested that a small hole drilled into it in-

Goddess with eyelashes made from broom bristles. Korelevu, Fiji. Photograph by Patrick Hodgson.

dicated that it had once been part of the regalia of a Fijian chief. Such Fijian chiefs as I number among my acquaintance are mystified. Never have they worn or seen such a one in their lives. Each, it is true, is the possessor of a golden cowry, a sign of royal birth, in which his spirit hovers and will continue to hover after his demise, but that is a different affair altogether. Anyway, as already explained, it is the egg cowry, chosen perhaps for its milk-white porcelain finish, that is the ceremonial shell and is attached to all regalia.

75

The Korolevu hotel boasts a public relations officer, one Hector Macdonald, the leading entrepreneur of the golden cowry, who is reputed to know who is hiding what where. Pat buys a shapely but somewhat anemic specimen from him, which Hector seems to prize so highly that he is reluctant to part with it. He maintains that golden cowries turn up on the reef only at the rate of about three in two years. How then, inquires Pat, does he account for the fact that we have obtained four in the last three weeks? Hector seems to require notice of this question, to which we think we can supply the answer. Namely, there are more golden cowries stashed away in a yard of silk on the islands than anyone dreams of, and Walai's ear is perhaps more attuned than Hector's to the Fijian bush telegraph. Meanwhile, a London friend of ours has written to a leading citizen in Suva asking him to help us buy a golden cowry. At this point I am summoned to an obsolete telephone like a black daffodil and, cowry in hand, I take the call leaning against the reception desk. It is the leading citizen himself, infinitely regretting that at the moment golden cowries are unobtainable. He has, however, put us down for one on a waiting list, but there are fifty names before ours.

The day of reckoning has overtaken us. It is the day on which our shells suddenly start to stink. Cairns of them adorn our balcony or are drawn up in neat rows on the chest of drawers. Starfish, sea fern, and seaweed lie drying upon the windowsill, while in the garden, under a brassica tree, three separate treasure troves are in different stages of decomposition, with a fourth under the night-blooming cereus. Walai is supposed to be superintending the cleansing of yet others in distant Vatua, for which he declines reward quite rightly, as he hasn't touched them. Have we then to spend this last radiant day combing through the catch, smelling each shell before it is packed, cleaning as we go, and isolating those which fail to make the grade? I fear we do. Pat spends three malodorous hours in the bathroom with them, then hands over the knife to me whereupon I spend two more; well, one, but it seems like two. The univalves have not yet sufficiently disintegrated to be dislodged, although some are beginning to leak around their apertures. These we hermetically seal up in a biscuit tin. The rest are immured in plastic bags except for the fragile ones, which are tenderly encased in cigarette cartons. We stow the lot in two rush baskets, liberally sprinkling the lot with Caron's Sweet Pea.

I never thought to see the night when Pat would dine wrapped in a scarlet sulu surmounted by a jade shirt overprinted with pineapples. Behind his right ear he wears a plumeria, around his neck a lei of coconut beans. Unself-conscious as a bulbul on a bough, he is even interpreting the dance music freely, instead of firmly sitting out awaiting a quickstep, vintage 1940. This is to be positively our last Fijian entertainment. By now every choric chant is as familiar to us as "Rule Brittania," and our table is sited as far out on the perimeter as we can get. We are joined by an Australian with an elderly wife, a presence in a mini-skirt, barefooted, with a camelia in her topknot. This citizen of Boologooro is a student of Bacchanalia. She conducts the band; she dances a solo; she yodels from the rostrum. She ends up flat on the dance floor with Flint, a dignified Alsatian dog, encased within her octopus embrace. Bill Clark, the kind hotelier, a shade uncertain of how to dispose of her, glides around the periphery. She grips him by the knees as he passes in a sort of rugger tackle. "Holy cod," she bawls when she has brought him down—a neat job—"I wouldn't be dead for quids, would you, mate?"

4 The Yasawa Isles

Ninety miles to the northwest of Korolevu lies the port of Lautoka, from which we are to embark on a jaunt through the Yasawa archipelago, a cluster of dependent islands north of Viti Levu. The drive is memorable chiefly for the suffocating dust that, trailing behind us in a pennant like vapor from a jet, penetrates the ultimate crannies of the body. The road snakes its way in between plump fields of coral pink earth, down to cobalt blue bays trimmed with white fringes of sand, and up again into wine red mountains inhabited only by an occasional herd of wild horses. In spite of the drought, which has remained unbroken around Lautoka, the city is redolent of sugar and spice and all things nice. The quays are given over to mills and warehouses piled high with kegs and bales of sweet-scented cargo. We are housed in an annex between a rum factory and a depository. Our bedroom is like a dungeon giving on to a cement wall. The only literature available to Pat with which to speed the passing hours when he is near suffocation is the Holy Bible in Fijian and English. It is some years since he has had recourse to the wisdom of Solomon, but by breakfast time he is resonant with exhortations from Ecclesiastes and the Proverbs, from which we form the impression that some of the early bards got their facts wrong. For instance:

"Can one go upon burning coals and his feet not be burned?" The unsought answer to this rhetorical question is surprisingly "Yes, in Fiji he can." In the island of Baqa they do almost nothing else, and if we had stayed in Korolevu until next Friday we

78

should have seen them doing it in the pit behind the laundry.

"The Lord chasteneth those whom he loveth." This aphorism provokes Pat. He is being chastened to the limit of his endurance by pains in the back at present but does not consider them to be a sign of esteem from Jehovah, with whom he is barely on nodding terms.

Meanwhile, saffron-robed processions on their way to some center of worship are soft-stepping through the streets, for this is the time of year when Hindus are also fire walking in honor of the goddess Kali. The climax is reached on the final day of a festival of intense religious fervor. Consecrated by nine days of purification rites, which include sticking needles through his cheeks and stabbing himself with a dagger, each devotee is now approaching the crucial test of the power of his own

Saffron-robed processions on their way to some center of worship are soft-stepping through the streets, for this is the time of year when Hindus are also fire-walking in honor of the Goddess Kali. Lautoka, Fiji.

enlightenment. The priests hold up effigies of the goddess and, to the accompaniment of the hypnotic throbbing of goatskin drums, they chant a summons to cross and recross a pit of red-hot coals to each barefooted young man. Apparently they respond with noble nonchalance, invariably performing the rite without flinching.

In contrast, Fijian fire walking is more of a *meke*, or a traditional exercise in asceticism and skill; and when, on a later visit, we witness one of these ceremonies, we are utterly convinced of their authenticity. At the moment both parties alike are engaged in making violent protests in the press against the exploitation of their ritual by tour promoters, who regard them as a sort of cabaret turn.

Next morning, feeling like characters out of a Somerset Maugham story, we board the *Ramanda*, a narrow eighty-tonner, rolling ominously in the pellucid waters of the tidal basin. The skipper is later to confess with endearing candor that she was built during the war as a patrol vessel for speed, and never mind the comfort. For instance, any sunbather reclining on the upper deck would at the first hint of a swell simply slide into the sea, for there is no guardrail. The cabins are trimmed to the bone. A thin foam pallet covers each unsprung berth, upon which sheets are so contrived that they wind like a sari round the human frame. Each passenger is rationed to one hook and a small drawer, while the plumbing tends towards unorthodoxy. When the basin plug is withdrawn, the water falls upon the unsuspecting feet beneath, to drain eventually into an aperture in the corner. Water rains from the shower indiscriminately upon the just and the unjust, over bather, basin, and loo, en route for the same corner. The loo has frankly given up.

Fortunately, we have been warned to bring the minimum of gear and have condensed ourselves into suitcases designed to fit under an airplane seat. So it is with considerable enjoyment that we watch a motorcade of affluent-looking Australians arriving from the Fijian Hotel with their possessions. A mountain of matching luggage, beauty boxes, shoe cases, transistors, and a battery of cameras are conveyed below deck by a team of sweating porters to quarters humbler even than our own.

The *Ramanda* off the Yasawa Isles. Photograph by Nitin Lal, Fiji Visitors Bureau.

Now it so happens that fate has not previously exposed either Pat or me to the Australian. Seen en bloc at the Korolevu, we seemed to have no particular message for one another. When eighteen passengers gradually assembly on the aft deck, where for the next week we are to pass our waking hours, it becomes evident that, except for a couple from Vienna, all hail from Australia, fair and free. A chill of foreboding is dispelled by the arrival of the captain on the deck. Aged about thirty-five, blond, and as blue-eyed as I presume Apollo to have been, he is not only startlingly handsome but commands instant devotion.

"I'm your skipper. My name's Rob. That's what you call me. Not captain or sir. Just Rob. I'll get you where we're goin' and back again or bust, and I want you all to have a damn good time. We're a mixed bag—always are on these trips. But if you just show each other the real niceness you've already shown me, we'll all get along fine. I'm comin' round now to ask you your first name and where you're from, and that's all we want to know. No need to wear anything but a bathing suit. Throw away your shoes. Only three rules. No liquor in your cabins. No sunbathing on the top deck. Don't give the kids anything when you go ashore or you'll turn 'em into beggars. For the moment they don't expect anything. Above all, don't give 'em sweets. There's not a single dentist on the islands and we don't want 'em to acquire the taste. Now, what's your name? Marlene? From Melbourne? And yours? . . ."

I do not know what alchemy there is in these guileless words, but by the time we have finished an incomparably better luncheon than any so far experienced in Fiji, no shade of tension lingers on board anywhere. We look into one another's eyes with laughter, accepting wholly everything we see. The spell is to hold throughout the trip.

Meanwhile, rocking violently in the wake of every passing dinghy, we lurch off among the spice boats, bound for the open sea. The first few hours of the voyage are agreeably occupied in sorting one another out. The Austrians, Louis and Hertha Bergmann, have emigrated to the United States where he is a specialist in nervous disorders, particularly in Parkinson's disease. As we surmised, the rest are all from Australasia. Julie, although she looks like an acrobat, turns out to be a nursing sister; Harold is a mining engineer; Tony a garage owner; Bob runs a pub; Jack is a ranch hand; and Bill owns a store. It takes a day or two longer to assign Shirley, Marlene, Eveline, Valerie, Tracy, and a brood of moppets and perishers to their correct menfolk.

Harold seats himself beside me in the bow. "One thing I can't stick is anyone who's stuck up."

"So?"

"Now take these royal visits." He eyes me firmly as if my hand was already in the till taking them. "With due respect to you, your Queen's right stuffy. That last visit was one God Almighty flop. She reads all her guff, and the whole job's done in aid of the brass hats, anyway. Lousy press they got. Trouble is, the advice they get is all crook. Philip tries to break loose— he knows what's what—but the way the setup is, it can't be done. I guess Charles is right enough—but he was just a sprog when he was here. Fact is, Australia looks to the Yanks now—they're the only ones that'll raise a finger when the blow falls." (We are to hear plenty about this impending blow.)

True-blue emotions charge around my system like yeast working in a vat. Rule Britannia. Something or other in Latin. *Ich dien.*

"So what would you have the Queen do if you were advising her?"

"Get out among the folks!" cries Harold robustly. "Get high! Kick off her shoes and dance the hokey-pokey in the sand with the blokes!"

This needs thinking about. "That would certainly be unstuffy," I say slowly at the end of the think, "and you personally might like it, Harold, but there are lots who wouldn't, and you might even be among them."

"What d'you mean I wouldn't like it? I'd love it."

"Well, the Queen's job is to be royal and, whatever your press may say, Harold, that's exactly what she is. Any cretin can dance the hokey-pokey."

"In Australia there's talk of a republic."

"Also in Glamorgan, West Fife, Holland, and Sweden, but more urgently at the moment there's a fish on the line behind you."

Can Harold have had access, do you suppose, to the deliberations in Buckingham Palace that preluded the Queen's walkabouts, Princess Anne's bloody hat blowing off in the hellish breeze, and Prince Philip's recommendation to the press to "stop running about like blue-arsed flies?" What could be less stuffy than these, Harold, wherever you may be?

Land is now sighted. Upon the wheelhouse floor slumbers a Fijian sailor, the steering wheel turning silently beside him as if guided by a spectral hand. A shove from Rob recalls him to his responsibilities, and soon we are being rapturously greeted at Waya Yalobi by a throng of voluble islanders, headed by an immaculate New Zealander, Trevor Withers, in a boating jacket and well-pressed flannels. His house, set in a neat shell-studded garden, stands twenty yards from where we wade ashore. It is basically a native *bure* which, with the addition of windows and what are known as conveniences, has been made as snug as any little gray home in Weston-Super-Mare. Dedicated Fijian attendants are catering to his every whim, and we think, but not for long, of our own domestic arrangements, now at a nadir. Mr. Withers has a house for guests nearby and a yacht equipped for big game fishing that rides at anchor in the lagoon, giving the impression that the white man's burden is not without its compensations. And where does the only foreigner on the island get a British military haircut?

The ocean, the domed sky, and even the starfish are cobalt blue, the water as warm as a caress. I roll and wallow in it, swimming under water with open eyes and lips and floating hair, cleansing myself of yesterday's scouring dust.

Unidentifiable shells gleam from the ocean bed among intricate clusters of marine vegetation varying between hard seaweed and soft coral, delicate as filigree, whose potential as material for pictures bemuses me almost to drowning point.

The island of Nanuya is our next objective and by dusk we are anchored off a sickle of white sand encircled by black motionless trees. Before disembarking to dine on shore, Rob assembles the company on the aft deck where, with nonchalant dexterity, he swaths each woman in a length of gaudy cotton and dishes out sulus to all the men. Flowers appear in clusters, around the neck, behind the ear, tucked in clinging furls of cotton, threaded through the hair. Rum on the house is then issued, as if we were about to go into action.

Huge fires are leaping and crackling on shore and from a grove rises a blend of guitars, ukeleles, and sweet falsetto voices. Within a clearing enclosed by low benches is grouped a clutch of Fijians, beflowered in chaplets and leis, singing to one another as if they were alone and in love. Shafts of moonlight strike through a canopy of palms. The royal blue sea lies motionless, slung upon the sand like a satin cloak. Two of the crew arrive to set up a bar, soon the source of a flowing brook of passion-fruit juice laced with rum. An appetite-provoking smell of pork threads its way through the trees. Suddenly, without forethought, we are all dancing barefoot in the clearing. All, that is to say, except Pat and Louis, who sit on a log discussing income tax. Sometimes we dance in twos, often in

The glory of Bengal (*Gloria Bengalensis*) and the glory of the seas (*Conus gloriamaris Chemnitz*), two of the rarest shells in the world. Photograph by Sara Heaton.

Fluted clams, found by Patrick Hodgson on Djardini Beach, Kenya. Photograph by Sara Heaton.

We decided to set aside a room in our house to enjoy the enchanting beauty of the shells. Photograph by Patrick Hodgson.

Our particular fancy, the teahouse at Goodwood House, built in 1739 by the duchess of Richmond and Gordon and her two daughters. Photograph by Geoffrey Harper. Copyright: The Trustees of the Goodwood Collection.

No one had prepared us for the staggering beauty of Tahiti. Photograph by Patrick Hodgson.

The decor is all Tahitian, the plumbing, happily, American. Hotel Tahara'a, Papeete, Tahiti. Photograph by Martha Hodgson.

Opposite the Pioneer Inn, the whalers' resort, was to be seen the *Carthaginian*, now, alas, at the bottom of the sea. Maui, Hawaii. Photograph by Patrick Hodgson.

At Everglades, the Greek sponge fishing fleet is in. West Florida. Photograph by Patrick Hodgson.

It became apparent that I had to find a studio. Photograph by Patrick
Hodgson.

The Wedding Party by Martha Hodgson. Photograph by Martha Hodgson.

"Coquillages" by Martha Hodgson, shown at the Upper Grosvenor Galleries, London. Photograph by Peter Waugh.

Sea Flowers by Martha Hodgson. Photograph by Patrick Hodgson.

Design for a Sanctuary by Martha Hodgson. Photograph by Martha Hodgson.

threes—Rob never has less than a girl on each arm—swinging together and apart, slinging away one partner and gathering up another. We are interrupted by a bird cry from the cooks to summon us to the fire where the dinner has attained concert pitch. Fish straight from the sea have been split open, spread upon a bank of embers, and covered over with layers of sacking saturated in sea water. When these are peeled off, a dish is revealed of the most tender texture and splendid flavor imaginable. Chicken, suckling pig, yams, sweet corn dripping in butter, pineapple, and bananas follow in full-flavored succession. Meanwhile the tempo of the music grows more urgent and, drawing close to the throbbing musicians, we join in as best we can. Julie, for instance, can sing in Maori. The solo·ist is now singing with closed eyes, his cheek resting on his own shoulder, the incarnation of suffering.

> Lash nye asi lay onmi peelo,
> Lash nye asi lay onmi bed,
> Lash nye asi lay onmi peelo
> I dreamed that my Bonny was dead

Until the climax in the last line, I imagined myself to have been singing miraculously in Fijian.

Perhaps the cuisine on Nanuya Levu imposes an undue strain upon the digestive systems of the guests, for most of them spend a short night but an unmerry one engaged in an unequal struggle with the ship's plumbing. As a consequence there is close competition for seats in the first boat ashore soon after daybreak. By 8 A.M. the entire complement of the *Ramanda* has disembarked and is invisibly pursuing its lawful occasions.

The reefs on this island are mercifully less formidable than those of Viti Levu. This particular beach, glowing like a flower garden, shelves steeply into a gentian sea and is starred over with miniature violet cowries, lemon yellow clams, and sprigs of flame coral. Pat finds a lady's curl shell like a porcelain corkscrew, a parody of a worm that is actually a marine snail. The tide begins to fall, and a few primitive boats hollowed out from tree trunks lie stranded on the shore. All is silence except for the whooping of a bird (the hoopoe?) and a distant snarling.

85

But is it so silent? All around is the swish and tinkle of water as little marine creatures dart to and fro, the soft crunch of a thousand tiny jaws, and the snap and crackle of the endless struggle between the eater and the eaten. ("Of course," said Lady Gwendolen, "all my family were Eton." "Good gracious, were they? Who by?")

Our next destination some hours further north is the island of Nabukeru. A considerable village edges the shore, at the extreme limit of which looms what is apparently an outsize boiler house. The primary—in fact, the only—industry here is copra, and this structure turns out to be the drying unit. The islanders will work only when money is needed for sensible reasons, such as boat materials, medical stores, or basic food like salt, sugar, and flour. When supplies of these begin to run low, a concerted effort is made. Copra—the flesh and the brown membrane of the coconut—is gathered in great quantities, bunged into the bakehouse, dried through by a fire made from the shells and fiber, and exported to make margarine, cattlefood, lipstick, soap, and face cream. A communal store then issues goods to those who collected copra in proportion to the quantity each has put into the oven.

The pride of Nebukeru is the Methodist church, from the Gothic windows of which a murmur like bees among clover blossom announces that all are occupied with the Lord's Prayer. At the end of the service Rob personally conducts us around. Gamboge linoleum gleams upon the floor, the highly polished pews are carved in yellow fumed oak, and on each window sill a tin can riots with trails of wild orchid. At the east end hangs a simple cross with a whale's tooth suspended from it by a piece of string. Fijians are indeed children of God and they attend divine service with fervor on Sundays and Wednesdays. Rob claims they have sessions of black magic on Saturdays to be on the safe side, and that it all fits in perfectly.

Several generations of the same family awaits us on the porch and lead the way in procession to their bure, where, instructed by Rob, the guests file in to the left and sit upon the floor. Our hosts, ranging in age from six months to ninety-one years, sit facing us on the right-hand side. We grin amiably at each other. Rob first makes an introductory speech in Fijian, evidently describing Western customs and aims to them, for they look at us in surprise and with some concern. Now speaking in English, Rob explains that every village is self-governing, that the wealth of the village is communal. Fijian families normally number no more than two or three children. The old, the young, and the sick are cared for by the whole community. Loneliness and insecurity are unknown. The Fijian tongue has, in fact, no words for them. At this point I am seized by violent cramp and, experiencing insecurity to the maximum, I peer urgently round for a means of retreat. Clearly there are no conveniences, ancient or modern, in this bure. It is surrounded, moreover, by an open-plan village and by several hundred villagers each watching our smallest movement with fascinated attention, punctuated by bursts of hilarity. It is a dilemma which offers few alternatives. With as much dignity as the situation admits, I rise suddenly, interrupting Rob, who is in full spate, and pop the vital question. Where? A graceful girl is delegated to conduct me down the main street to a grass hut on the outskirts of the village, set apart as if in quarantine. The population watches the procession in respectful silence, as if I were being led to the scaffold. The door is shut firmly behind me leaving me in total darkness, but not, fortunately, before I have caught a glimpse of a deep cemented shaft covered by a grid, like the one under which unlucky John the Baptist is battened down in the final act of *Salome*.

A boy with a basket is squatting in the shade of the hut when I emerge. He lifts its lid with a dazzling smile, holding up five fingers.

"Five cents each." These key words prove to be his entire vocabulary in English. I look with astonishment into the basket, which contains half a dozen or so chambered Nautiluses in mint condition, soup no doubt having been made from every fragment of the late lamented squids. This graceful cephalopod, cousin to the octopus and the cuttlefish, contains within its scroll about thirty gas chambers, linked together with geometric perfection, which balance and propel it through the water. It is, in fact, the prototype of the modern submarine named after it. A combative loner, it ranges the ocean depths at several thousand feet, surfacing to feed only at night, thus

The chambered nautilus contains within its scroll about thirty gas chambers, linked together with geometric perfection, which balance and propel it through the water. The argonaut that forms the paper-thin calciferous boat-shaped shell makes it only as a container of her eggs. Photograph by Sara Heaton.

Section of the chambered nautilus and sea horses. A combative loner, the chambered nautilus ranges the ocean depth at several thousand feet, surfacing only to feed at night. Photograph by Sara Heaton.

being a rare acquisition for the sluggard collector. To the stupefaction of the boy, I instantly acquire his whole stock. With a
whoop of triumph he leaps off, to reappear, posthaste, displaying an argonaut in one hand and leading two grinning children
by the other.

"Five cents each." (Would fifteen cents buy it plus the kids?)
The argonaut forms a paper-thin calciferous boat-shaped shell
only as a container for her eggs. Once the young are hatched
out, the shell floats at random on the ocean face, empty as a
bubble. An early but fanciful engraving shows the argonaut
being propelled onward by means of two leaflike sails and several oarlike arms.

The reef here, which gradually emerges as the tide recedes,
teems with every sort of aquatic life. Pat practically treads on
a long silvery snake at which he takes a poke with his stick;
it whips off with a flick and a wink of water. Scarlet aster starfish, violet jellyfish, spider starfish, scuffling burrow crabs, sea
urchins with spikes like black spears, and shoals of darting
harlequin fish animate the pools. As I gaze into the depths
in search of shells, I seem to hear the voice of Bill Ryan, a
white hunter with whom we once went on safari. "Don't look
at things, look *into* them," he used to say. "And *look* before
you set down your feet. Watch the elephant, for God's sake.
You town dwellers never walk light and true, like the elephant."

Well, I must have been walking fairly light and true lately
or by now I should have at least broken a leg, for nothing
exists more lethal to walk on than coral coated with slime.

Rob is reticent about the next stop. Is there perhaps something up his sleeve?

"What's the name of the next place?"

"I've forgotten."

"What time shall we get there?"

"I don't know."

"Well, what time is it now?"

"I haven't the slightest idea."

It is not long, however, before we are within the encircling
arm of a promontory of the volcanic island of Sawa-i-lau, whose
precipitous face, distorted by weird outcrops of rock, is about

as welcoming as a mad dog. We land upon a flinty beach and climb a hempen ladder dangling from an overhanging cliff. The prospect of this enterprise eliminates several starters. A shale track leads to a steep descent between overhanging crags and into a dark ravine that eventually opens out into an immense cavern smelling of the tomb and filled with steely black water. We have come prepared to bathe and, although the prospect is not inviting, one by one we subside gingerly into its oleaginous embrace. Protesting shrieks and splashes echo and expand in the gloom-ridden dome overhead. The Wagnerian scene is now joined by Rob with two of his crew, Chandra and Toma, who surface among the swimmers like seals, beckoning us onward towards the cavern wall. Here Rob is seized by the hair, his head pressed smartly downward, and he submerges without a bubble. Crescent-shaped grins are turned toward us.

"Who next?"

After a few seconds of stunned silence, a distant bellow from Rob disturbs a new range of echoes in a deeper key. Where's he got to? Beyond lies a second cavern, entirely enclosed except for this submerged entrance under a bar of rock. Chandra and Toma now seize us, one by one. Shriek, gurgle, glug! Down we go. Rob's waiting arm draws his victims under the bar and upward while he utters demoralizing banshee howls and hollow groans.

A dashing boat trip follows among some spooky rock formations, greatly enjoyed by Chandra who conducts it but less appreciated by those of us in clammy swimsuits who are in no mood to admire the geological strata.

After dinner we sail back to Kabukeru, where an entertainment in our honor is being prepared in the meetinghouse. This is presided over by the Ratu Epeli, whose every feature is stamped with lines of benignant authority. He is a striking figure, standing six-foot-six in his bare feet and arrayed in all the glory of Solomon. No major domo of the marines could bear himself with greater elegance or distinction nor hold such absolute command over his troupe of singers and dancers. All previous performances look in comparison like Pierrot shows. The dancers themselves are like black pearls, like swans, like naiads—as remote and pure as the original Sylphides. Louis

Bergman's researches lead him—the clod—to conclude that the dominating influence at work is probably not so much purity as the Methodist minister.

Pat and I ask the ratu's permission to distribute a sack of marbles we have brought ashore for the children. Warm brown bodies with clutching hands advance in a tidal wave into which I sink without a ripple. Pat is standing by, camera ready, but recognizes only occasionally a threshing elbow or foot, as in Eton's wall game. By the time we have restored order, meted out justice and comforted the comfortless (there are not enough marbles to go round), all the other guests have left with Chandra in the last boat. Also we have understood Rob's prohibition on presents for the children. With eyes riveted on the *Ramanda*'s lights, we stand ankle-deep in the navy blue sea, debating procedure if she sails without first counting heads. But Rob is less vague than he pretends to be. Presently he puts off in the lifeboat, approaching shore as if driving a Dodg'em. We bucket off in clouds of spray with Rob at the wheel, singing to the moon at the top of his voice. When I was a child I used to think the moon was God.

These islands are in the direct path of the hurricanes, which occur roughly every two years. For this reason the houses are lashed together with twine, their doors strategically placed so that, however much they bend and sway before the fury of the gale, the dwellings seldom collapse. But the village elders now wish to present a more modern image, and their thatch, so cosy in winter and cool in summer, and capable, moreover, of withstanding the elements, is being replaced with corrugated iron roofs, the twine with nails and the adobe with concrete. Rob has cautioned them that they will fry and freeze in due season and probably be blown into the bay, but disregarding all warnings they are blandly continuing the pursuit of progress, and recently Rob's gloomiest predictions have been realized. The full death roll has not yet been called following the latest calamitous hurricane. And what, you may ask, will be their next objective? The airstrip, no doubt, the high-rise hotel, and the package tour.

Now headed towards Lautoka in deteriorating weather, we collect two Colombian priests, a nun, and some suitcases off a deserted headland. All three have been proselytizing these islands for the last twenty years. Sister Mary Joseph of the Marian Order cannot exactly recall what her original function was intended to be, but it is now to heal, to doctor, to teach, to advise, and to bring to God.

"You know," she explains in a soft Cork accent, her cornflower eyes just one whit bluer than the sea around her, "once you have lived among these people it's nowhere else you can live, you see, and I pray to the Blessed Virgin that I may live here until I die."

Whitecaps are blowing in from the open sea when we put in for a last swim off the island of Nanuya Balavu. The receding tide discloses a spit of sand covered in eelgrass and crisscrossed with furrows. It is pierced with small bubbling holes, alive with invisible activity. Into one of these I plunge a hand and am startled when it closes upon a weed-clogged object like a petrified flower. I fling it down as if it would bite, when a movement of the operculum shows it to be alive—a *Murex nigritis*, about four inches long, the first I have found alive. Holding it aloft I ponder upon its antecedents. In the fifth century B.C., the inhabitants of Tyre and Sidon discovered that by pulverizing shell and creature together, and by subjecting them to endless boilings and purifications, a purple dye could be extracted from the *Murex purpura*, which was to become the hallmark of majesty and authority even to the present day. It is supposed to have taken three million such Murexes to produce each pound of dye. Alexander the Great found a hoard of purple cloth in the treasury of King Darius of Persia; Cleopatra went to war under purple sails; Roman emperors wore purple as a sign of their sovereignty; princes were "born to the purple"; and our own Queen Elizabeth advanced up the nave of Westminster Abbey to her annointing with a purple velvet train twenty yards long flowing from her shoulders.

These reflections are broken into by Bob, the pub owner from Sydney, with a plain and somewhat inconvenient daughter, Sandra, aged about nine, but an incipient entomologist if ever I saw one. They are looking for a third pair of hands. Two conspirators are needed to sneak up on each unsuspecting rock and overturn it between them while a third person darts in

93

to kill or to catch. The underside of the first rock reveals a microcosm of squirming life, including a long cupreous snake that whips out like a lash and makes off in a series of frantic S-turns. I am unable to suppress a small shriek. Shocked, Sandra straightens up, examining me contemptuously with a pale clinical eye. Reluctantly I see myself as she must surely see me, as one who prizes the jewel but who quails at the humble craftsman within, as a queasy presence who sickens at the touch of the cold-blooded and the small and slimy dead. Well, let's face it, Sandra, I'm plain squeamish and always have been. The frenzied struggles of hunted creatures horrify me. I pray that the shot will miss the pheasant, the salmon elude the hook. Wasps frequently live to sting my rescuing hand as they are fished from the swimming pool. In my garden I never cut one of two flowers growing conjugally together. But truth compels me to confess that the fate of the mollusks, in their last throes in the bag upon my arm, for some reason fails to arouse my compassion. Perhaps their very passivity exempts them from it. Nor am I now able to recall by exactly what processes I made this drastic transition from the Institute of Fine Arts into the Natural History Museum.

Rob, afer examining a John Piperish sky, has remarked mildly that dirty weather is blowing up, and as the *Ramanda*'s nose emerges from shelter it hits her with full force. The sky is charged with menacing slate gray clouds, while the sea has become a range of slowly advancing mountains. The convulsions of the *Ramanda* would be comic if they were not so alarming. As she corkscrews along, green water is shipped first on one gunwhale then on the other. Sea, sky, and islands rear and dip as if glimpsed while looping the loop. With one accord the passengers take to their bunks and hold on tight— that is to say, all but the Colombian fathers and Sister Mary Joseph who have no bunks and who are presumably somewhere below holding on to one another.

When calmer waters prevail near Lautoka, Louis Bergman comes to take leave of Pat and me. Throughout the voyage he has watched our shell-cleaning activities with detached interest. Now he picks up a particularly odoriferous *Conus planorbis*, a jolly fellow in honey and black porcelain, which he subjects

94

to a prolonged scrutiny. (I am still rinsing out this particular cone six months later.)

"There are, if I may say so, two better methods of extricating the creature from its shell than the ones I have seen you employing. The long-term one is simply to steep them in cold water in a sealed jar to encompass the smell, and bacteria will gradually dispose of the animal. Alternatively, you can stand them in a jar to which you add one teaspoonful of formaldehyde to a quarter of a pint of cold water. This will pickle the animal so that he will not disintegrate. You can then draw him out whole with your curved surgical forceps."

Happy thought, Prof. That's just what we'll do with our curved surgical forceps the minute we get to Tahiti.

5 Tahiti

Before parting on the quay, the entire cast of the *Ramanda* fervently exchange addresses, vowing to visit one another in Toowoomba, Wagga Wagga, Upper Hutt, Moosup (Connecticut), and, I freely admit, South Kensington, London. But it's not as easy as you might think to disengage yourself at Lautoka and instantly attain distant climes. A twenty-four-hour interval is to elapse before the ship's party is able to dispose of itself. The chill wind that blows through the sparse marble halls of the Fijian airport motel in which we are marooned is not merely climatic. The nub of the problem is pithily expressed by Jack, until yesterday my resolute admirer. No doubt the penetrating quality of his voice is a matchless asset back home on the range.

"It'll be a right cow," we hear him trumpeting into the ear of Mrs. Cathcart, the hotel proprietor, "if those bloody Pommies ever hole in at Toowomba base."

Mrs. Cathcart is herself one of those bloody Pommies, who holed in at Fiji base years ago and somehow got assimilated. But her voice retains the burr of Caledonia and of distant lochs, and our own encounter with her turns out to be a lucky one. For our plane to Tahiti remains unaccountably in New Caledonia many chains hence. Instead of waiting for it stranded on a hard bench in the departure lounge, we loll in a sitting room provided by her kindness, restoring morale by an occasional dip in the pool.

The South Pacific Games have been taking place this week in New Guinea. When the plane finally touches down, it reveals a babbling freight of Tahitian athletes in full rig of scarlet track suits, smothered in medals, bedecked with plumes, roses, and pennants, and thrumming on guitars. We press in amongst the turmoil and find seats in the tail next to a deadpan Chinese Tahitian, Min Pao or Pin Mao by name, the winner of a gold medal for sumo wrestling and, in his spare time, a dentist. It is 3 A.M. when, with every voice raised in jubilant song and all stops pulled out on the string instruments, we float into Papeete airport to a tumultuous welcome. Each hero is kissed and embraced by both sexes alike, loaded with yet more leis and wreathed with tiaras, the national flower. Neither the rejoicing nor the lateness of the hour, however, deflects the customs staff from commandeering all the luggage from Fiji in order to fumigate it for a couple of hours in a gas chamber. ("Any gold bullion, diamonds, narcotics, obscene literature, fruit, feathers, beetles, or dried meat?") This intervention is irresolutely received by the jaded passengers, who have been keenly anticipating their beds. But all our problems are solved by an urbane figure in a chaplet of white roses who, after encircling each exasperated neck with a lei of tiaras, announces his intention of driving us to the Tahara'a Hotel in his taxi and returning later for our baggage. Hand luggage for some reason being exempt, he picks up ours—two baskets of shells—and we follow our benefactor towards a toothbrushless and naked night, but no matter. Only later do we discover that the palm trees of Fiji are being exterminated by a rhinoceros beetle and that the officials are, reasonably enough, seeking to exclude them from Tahiti. We look speculatively at our two baskets, heaving all too plainly with grubular activity.

Nobody has prepared us for the staggering beauty of Tahiti. Lofty violet and viridian mountains drop sheer to the shore; cascades of blossoms, in astonishing variety and color, weep and creep over every house, wall, bank, and tree, and over each adorable curve of every Tahitian body. We catch glimpses of fine-boned men, majestic women, and entrancing children, in beflowered peaked hats, crowns, bracelets, and anklets. The

We might be drifting endlessly through some extensive botanical garden. Tahiti. Photograph courtesy of French Embassy.

Hotel Tahara'a drops in terraces down the face of a cliff over-hanging the sea, each room set behind an embowered balcony. Waterfalls and running brooks thread their way between minia-ture gardens, a swimming pool, intimate bars, shady niches from which to contemplate the view, and elegant boutiques. The decor is all Tahitian, the plumbing, happily, 100 percent Ameri-can.

The wrestler, Mr. Pao or Mao, had confided to me on the plane that Tahiti was paradise before They destroyed it. "Their" identity was not established, but I assume the deterioration began when Captain Samuel Wallace, in H.M.S. *Dolphin*, dis-covered Tahiti in 1767 and raised the British standard here. The following year, Captain Bougainville, unaware of Captain Wallace's existence, also discovered it and claimed it for France. The next year brought Captain Cook on the first of three visits to the island, when he made his famous observations of the transit of Venus. In 1788 Captain Bligh of the *Bounty* paid a brief call, followed a year later by his mutinous crew, who in the meantime had set the poor captain adrift in a longboat.

It seems that before the advent of the sea captains and, worse still, of the missionaries who were to have so disastrous an effect upon the Tahitians, the islands enjoyed an existence of almost unbroken felicity. To the Tahitian every action was a prayer and life itself a continuous sacrament. A supreme deity dominated their dancing, wrestling, hunting, fishing, swimming, and loving. He was manifest in the sky and the sea, the wind and the earth, and the creatures thereof. This was a frame of mind intolerable to the missionaries, who energetically set about eradicating it and substituting instead their own unrelenting white God.

In 1779 a minor chief, Hapai by name, backed enthusiastically by the missionaries, established the Pomare dynasty, which was to last for nearly a hundred years. Massacres, corruption, and death through venereal and other diseases were the sorry harvest of this regime. It is enough to say that in 1768 Captain Cook estimated the population at 200,000; By 1803 it was 5,000. The last sovereign, Pomare V, turned over the kingdom to France. He lies in Arue, buried all too suitably under an outsize Benedictine bottle. What inhabitants now remain are a mixture of Polynesian and Chinese, with a French governor and troops in Papeete. The Polynesians occupy themselves in the production of copra, vanilla, and coffee, and in fishing and diving for mother-of-pearl, while, as elsewhere, the Chinese keep shop and run the commerce.

We are waylaid in a courtly manner by a well-sprung man in a formal suit of such neatness that a white camellia behind his ear gives him a slightly indecorous look. He introduces himself as the hotel manager, Charles Klemes from Czechoslovakia, whose mission it is to change this island from a place of transit to a port of destination. At present he confesses that the outlook is hazardous. Why? Perhaps nature has been too good to these people, for life here is so delightful that they positively decline to work. A waiter, for instance, who has been in his employ for months, simply does not turn up one morning, not even to collect his back pay. He is seen in Papeete riding a Vespa, wearing a European suit and a crown of pink roses. It is to buy this Vespa that he has been working, and until he needs something else he will not do so again.

"How then can I run a hotel?" He gives a shrug that personifies all mystification.

Papeete (pronounced Pa-pay-tay) is a pastiche composed of a decrepit shantytown and a bustling seaport. A long wharf, beside which unrolls a shadeless thoroughfare, is proliferating ancient buses and cars, boneshaking bicycles, and barefooted pedestrians. A row of open-end booths faces a line of scruffy freighters and junks, restless in the swell. Running parallel to the quay is the spinal column of the town, which contains an informal-looking hospital, a cosy jail, and a couple of hermetically sealed banks. It radiates outward into back streets of steaming laundries, bakeries, and cafés, to vociferous printing presses, to the market, and to a ruminative native life. In one direction, among boutiques, supermarkets and incipient skyscrapers, the pace sharpens and the click of high heels, the jangle of bangles, and the roar of pop music sound along the boulevard. But in the other a tide of vegetation is gradually submerging the half-collapsed dwellings, where the Tahitians are variously deliberating, sleeping in the shade, weaving flowers together, playing with children, or communing with birds in pagodalike cages.

We board a bus and roar down the mountainside like train robbers. Ever since breakfast Pat has been with difficulty suppressing a secret, one calculated to turn any collector of shells sea green with envy. Somewhere in Papeete West, it seems, there exists an expert cleaner, polisher, and, I fear, a decorator and engraver of shells. The last craftsman in this particular field in London was gathered a couple of years ago. In the market square we pick a Chinese taxi driver with an archaic smile and an all-seeing eye. Pat asks at a venture if he knows a Mr. Itchener?

"You know Mr. Itchener?"

"I don't, but do you?"

We have not misjudged our man. "I take you to him."

On the outer fringe of the town in a clapboard house almost extinguished by bushes of brilliantined leaves, we find Mr. Itchener and his wife, Ray, leisurely savoring their roses. Their front lawn is occupied by a small shop beyond which, in a cloud of nacreous dust, stands a whirring workshop, where eight men are working lathes with which they cut, scale, polish, and buff the shells to whatever extent is necessary. Huge baskets piled high with the products of their industry beam and bloom in immaculate radiance. Beneath an avocado tree, a boy with a bucket of decomposing shells is patiently purging them with the aid of a scalpel and some forceps. Mr. Itchener himself is in poor shape, having almost cut off his thumb with a circular saw, but, rallied by our enthusiasm, he agrees to give our Fijian catch precedence over his other work. He promises to skin and expurgate at least some of them before we leave at the end of the week.

Ray is not one to let orchids grow under her feet. She cuts our gratitude short by pointedly confronting us with their own wares. The shelves of her shop glitter with shell jewelry in varying degrees of taste, with ghastly lamps, ashtrays, and figures, and some musical instruments with whose werewolf howling we are all too familiar. The spectacle of many splendid shells stripped of their periostracum and decorated with tawdry designs somewhat shakes our confidence. But Mr. Itchener calls upon heaven to witness that no shell of ours shall be sullied by any hand bent upon improving on nature. No engraved palm trees. No hula dancers. No inscriptions. On this understanding I buy a huge abalone etched with a Greek key design, a bracelet made of nacre cut in a clever coil and, for our museum, a burnished shell converted into a lamp. Pat buys a crucifix for our Catholic cook, having forgotten she has gone with the wind. Ray encircles our necks with leis of heart cockles, and we part with expressions of mutual regard. A coconut whizzes down from aloft as we drive away, practically staving in the roof of the taxi.

It had been our intention to ignore the shell emergency fast developing in the farthest reaches of our balcony until we got back to London. Facts, however, now compel us to review the

101

position. In the time at his disposal, Mr. Itchener cannot tackle more than about half of our total hoard, and the other half is already crawling with unspeakable slugs. Also, the sealed tin is beginning to exude a lethal gas and the problem is how to get it to Mr. Itchener before it explodes. Pat races off with it and with a loaded basket emitting fumes of main drain, while I contend with the rest in the bathroom. A sickening scum and a smell of brimstone rises from each succeeding basinfull of water. By dusk both of us are overdue for a bit of gracious living. Bathed, annointed, and hung with flowers in appropriate places, we migrate to the Discovery Bar, said to be an exact replica of Captain Cook's living quarters. Had he, do you suppose, a bar consisting of an elongated grand piano padded with black plastic? On this a Tahitian pianist, wearing a necklace of shark's teeth, is accompanying a soprano whooping through the "Indian Love Call" in Norwegian. On a stool perches a native of Nebraska with a double row of teeth like a Tahitian deity, explaining that wherever she goes, she can't think why, chaps cluster all around her. (For the moment, actually, none are clustering.) Restored with champagne and with elbows planted on the piano top, now vibrating with "You forgot to remember," we fall into instant friendship with a couple from Santa Barbara, Jim and Ann Kernick-Cole. Jim, crisp as a potato chip in starched mess kit, looks perhaps somewhat stiff-necked, which in fact he is, having broken it when baling out of a plane during the Battle of Britain. Anne, some years his junior, looks like a jonquil in a glass of spring water, a deceptive impression since closer acquaintance proves her to be a notably earthy wit.

We join forces with them next morning, intending to fly to the Isle of Moorea, the fantastic volcanoes of which dominate the horizon. Christianity was first introduced into Polynesia on this island, which is described as yet another terrestial paradise. Ridges of leaden clouds and squalls of ferocious rain blot it from view, however, as we wait on the airstrip for an aircraft that never materializes. We settle for the paradise we already have and follow a stony track down to the beach, which curves enticingly, if duskily, below the hotel terrace. The path peters out in a glade commanded by a notice board bearing the single word "Tabu."

As we suspected, the beach consists of inky volcanic dust and lives down to all expectations. An abrasive wind drives sharp flint into our faces as we toil towards a reef about half a mile away. Shells have absented themselves. Not only is the coral reef coated in green slime but it is interspersed with purple sea urchins like porcupines. Blackened water tears past, diverting the foot from its objective. So ruffled are the pools by the force of the blast that it is impossible to examine them without bending double, in which posture the hat blows off. Dead pearly tops, mostly inhabited by hermit crabs, abound in this marine paradise but little else. Thus, it is not long before we are ready to pack it in, although to reach shore without a fracture will be a major achievement.

A sheltered cove is our objective, within which a Gauginesque group of three Tahitian girls is sitting under a tree pendulous with yellow blossom. While one combs out her waist-long hair, a second is twining tiaras into a snowy chaplet, and a third is slashing a coconut with a machete. They are waitresses from the Tahara'a—Victorine, Ea, and Sabina. When Pat asks if he may photograph them they giggle and demur, but nonetheless fall immediately into a frieze of both natural and statuesque elegance.

It continues to be our unshaken purpose to fly over the Sea of the Moon to Moorea but, although we all get up each morning in time for the plane, some sort of Tahitian miasma causes us to gravitate instead towards less exacting activities. The market, for instance, offers hampers of shells from all over the archipelago, including Moorea. Also a profusion of goods made from primary materials such as volcanic rock, coral, mother-of-pearl, bone, tooth, shells, feathers, and vegetable fibers. A tattooist is plying his trade in a booth. Tapa, baskets, hats, and bales of pareu, a hand-blocked material, are being bargained for by the grisly cargo from a cruise ship, who are unaware that all prices here are fixed. (There is also a total ban on tipping in Tahiti, which makes for a delightful freedom of communication between the waiter and the waited upon.) In spite of this throng of would-be patrons, the shutters of the Papeete shops all remain hermetically sealed between 11:00 A.M. and 2:30 P.M., a hiatus from which we rescue a forlorn Aus-

The market offers a profusion of goods made from primary materials, such as volcanic rock, coral, mother-of-pearl, bone, tooth, feathers, and vegetable fibers. Tahiti. Photograph courtesy of French Embassy.

tralian horse coper by inviting him to lunch. Three months ago he drew a winning number in a sweepstake and, never before having left Australia, he took straight off for Ireland, where he discovered he was a direct descendant from an ancient line of kings.

"How absolutely fascinating," I say, "which king?"

"Well," says he, "me name is Hogan."

Mr. Itchener's handiwork is delivered in a wicker basket. Death is a condition that becomes the luckless mollusk. He is his own splendid memorial. Would that our own efforts were equally gratifying. The losing struggle with the consignment in the bathroom is still in progress, and tomorrow we are to leave at daybreak. At each return to anchor, Pat pelts upstairs to give the shells a once-through with clean water in the washbasin. Every visit reveals khaki-colored water and a stupefying stench. Our packing problem also demands both ingenuity and a further purchase of palm leaf baskets, so after a few token gestures we procrastinate, setting forth instead on a tour of the island with the Kendrick-Coles. The expedition lacks bite. We might be drifting endlessly through some extensive botanical garden. For instance, where did Gauguin live? Well, his house has been burned down. What about Jean Jacques Laurent who owns the Museum of Artifacts? Alas, he left for New Guinea this morning. Didn't Robert Louis Stevenson live here? Yes, but his house has been pulled down. Any traces left by Captain Cook anywhere? The captain left no trace, unless you can call a plinth, erected to his memory on Venus Point, a trace, or a bamboo house, peopled with waxwork figures of the captain and his jolly henchmen, all bowing low before Tahitian ladies with flowers behind both ears.

Once more at the Tahara'a, Pat rushes up for an interim grapple with the shells before settling down to *maihais* (two kinds of rum, plus pineapple) out of tall green glasses off the padded piano. After the third *maihai* we decide not to pack until after dinner, for which we are to dress a la Polynèse for the last time. Pat is wrapped in his Fijian sulu with a frangipani

Each one thrums upon some hand-wrought instrument except for the rear-most, who beats rhythmically upon a soft drink bottle with a spoon. Tahiti. Photograph courtesy of French Embassy.

behind his ear and a lei of orchids, but he manages nevertheless to look undeniably male. Anne and I are tricked out in shell chaplets and earrings with carnation leis and bracelets, and feel, and we hope look, reasonably female. Jim crackles away in some sort of safari kit, all buttons and pockets.

Our table in a bay window looks over an ocean shining like opalescent oil in the moonlight. A band of ready-witted musicians, with tossing hair and swivelling hips, moves into the throb of the erotic *tumare* dance. Jim closes his eyes in ecstacy: "Bring on the dancing girls!" he breathes, and they bring them on.

Not that they actually dance. A single file of five jumbo ladies cocooned in cotton, like bolsters, and hung in plastic leis, winds slowly in between the tables chanting a dolorous dirge. Each one thrums upon some hand-wrought instrument, except for the rearmost who beats rhythmically upon a Coca Cola bottle with a spoon. They look like professional mourners in search of clients. Having delivered their complaint they fade from our vision to some lower level of the building where their voices thin out sadly into the evening air.

Deciding to pack when and if we go to bed at all, we are still restoring morale as best we may with *maihais* when the sky discloses a dawn of an unusually shoddy shade of pink, like a sunrise tellin shell.

The main boulevard leading from the airport into San Francisco is spanned by a neon sign: "Live ye it up." On the foundations of the ancient Spanish colonial town have risen steel-blade skyscrapers and shabby warehouses, dazzling shops, disreputable slums, and shocking smells. Exhilarating glimpses of the sea and of lush parks occur between gaps in the seven mountains upon which the city is built. Avalanches of fog pour daily into the low-lying parts of the city, leaving only the tips of the skyscrapers pricking into a viridian sky. All that we see of the famous Golden Gate bridge is the road unrolling ahead and, when we glance back, the red spires of the towers that carry its vast suspension. We spend the day sealed up in a sight-seeing bus, taking in everything from an early mission house to a late party in a Chinese dive. At night an ancient cable car, driven by a jolly motorman and hung all over with uninhibited customers, clangs down Hyde Street hill to Fisherman's Wharf. The scenes of disorder at the top, for it is Saturday night, make us shrink into our shells like the dry corpses of our own mollusks. While we are sustaining life in a packed fish bar overlooking the shrimp fleet, a minor earthquake occurs. The swaying chandeliers are totally ignored. For the last ten years everyone here has been expecting to be swallowed up by an earthquake, so why worry? Live ye it up.

Mountains of oysters and clams are being shucked and consumed on the spot by passersby, as well as scallops, crayfish, prawns and shrimps. Seashells from the fishing nets, piled high in lobster pots, are on sale at ten cents apiece. Among them are such rareties as the white ceremonial egg cowry, the Murex brassica, the bailer, and the left-handed lightning whelk. All are shining with internal cleanliness. A vision of untold hours passed in countless alien bathrooms passes like a pageant before the inner eye. We subject them to a long, considering scrutiny. It is an unsettling sign. For beneath the open window in our room in the St. Francis Hotel stand several baskets of shells purged almost to extinction by our industry, still odoriferous, still disgracefully leaking a rich brown feculence. The smell permeates the corridor, all our possessions, our very skin. It easily outdoes the puny efforts of the Madame Rochas scent with which they are now sprayed. Soon it will also permeate a London-bound jet, but of this forthcoming event our sky hostesses are for the moment blissfully unaware.

6 Maui

Into every life, they say, some rain must fall. Until the day previous to our arrival there, the Hawaiian Islands had been enjoying an unusually clement winter. After a night spent in flying steadily and rather boringly into a never-setting sun, we descend upon Honolulu through blinding rain and are conducted to a lesser runway to confront the plane that is to deliver us to our final destination, Maui. Six sodden figures wait passively on the tarmac beside an aircraft with the word Flea emblazoned upon its nose. This must be one of a special strain bred for island hopping. While the pilot, a flower child in a saffron tunic, is stowing the baggage (two suitcases in each wing and two in the nose), the passengers squeeze in, knees to chin, and the rest of the luggage is shoved in between their contorted limbs.

"Visibility nil. Heavy turbulence! Don't know if we can make it, but we can try," announces the pilot blithely.

We bucket off into a blanket of clay-colored cloud, with hail rattling on the fuselage like bullets. It is half an hour before land appears fleetingly through scudding cloud.

"Lanai," announces the pilot, "where Mr. Kamaki and Mr. Eka want to land. I shall circle a few times to see if I can break in—otherwise, gentlemen, you will have to come with us to Maui."

He drops between two banks of cloud like a knife thrust, and Messrs. Kamaki and Eka thankfully extricate themselves. A similar dart into Maui, during which I keep my eyes glued to a crossword puzzle, lands us neatly on a strip, once a road, now widened to accommodate the air service but still so narrow that the wings of the plane only just clear a burgeoning hedge on each side.

Beneath a tulip tree are posted three Mauian girls, long in the body, short in the leg, the owners of huge flat feet. With wide-boned faces and a black torrent of unadorned hair falling to the edge of skirts made from ti leaves, they look like startled buffalo. In contrast, four frilly females in muumuus—the Hawaiian version of the mother hubbard—are engaged in a vociferous hand of bridge in the airport office. One detaches herself, cards in hand, to telephone for a taxi. Only ill can come, she predicts darkly, from setting foot in the Sheraton Hotel, for which we are bound (three no trumps), for it stands upon a graveyard and is haunted by unquiet Mauian spirits. For the time being every palm tree in sight is bent double in a shrieking wind, while rain drives at right angles across our vision, so, while the cab driver prudently awaits a lull, Pat buys a Hawaiian phrase book. Their alphabet consists of twelve letters only, which, in addition to the vowels, are H, K, L, M, N, P, and W. A short list of indispensable words follows. These, it is suggested, are: alas, beloved, crooked, dead, dirty, drunk, free, forbidden, feast, insane, sacred, stupid, tomorrow, urine, trouble, woman, war, wind, and yawn. Pat feels this probably accurately describes the pitch.

A few weeks ago at a meeting of the Conchological Society at the Victoria and Albert Museum, the following sentence had decided for us the problem of a destination:

"There are a wide variety of mollusks, Professor Fistleton-Twines, to be found in the Hawaiian Islands."

It is now my intention to give a brief account of these islands, as it has been my lot since returning home to be met by a blank face at the mention of the word Maui, a lesser island in the group, for which we have plumped.

"Let's think," they ponder, almost to a man. "What was it before it was Maui?" (In spirit these innocents are always in Africa).

The Polynesian kingdom of Hawaii consisted of twenty islands of which, even now, only seven are inhabited, and it was discovered by Captain Cook in January, 1778. The islanders he found there were almost totally preoccupied with the worship of nature. Although One Supreme Being ruled over all, the gods with whom they were hourly concerned were the local ones of war, of the arts, of peace, of love, of growing things, and of departed spirits.

In Hawaii, Oahu, and Maui, the islands formed by volcanic eruption, Pele, the Goddess of Volcanoes, reigned supreme. But whatever the particular cult, all were animated by the cut and thrust of an interplay between Mana (supernormal power) and Kapu (the setting up of things forbidden).

Captain Cook explored in turn Kauai, remarkable for its record rainfall and for Somerset Maugham's *Rain;* Niihau, now inhabited only by Hawaiians of ancient stock and culture, and owned by a family called Robinson (Swiss, I presume); and Oahu, upon which lie Honolulu, Pearl Harbor, and Waikiki Beach. Later he visited Maui, the center of the whaling industry, Molokai, renowned for its scenery and its leper colony, and Hawaii, the largest of the group. He christened them the Sandwich Islands, after his patron, Lord Sandwich, and Mark Twain described them as "the loveliest fleet of islands that lie anchored in any ocean." In 1779 Captain Cook, having sailed safely away, put back again into Hawaii to shelter from a storm. A fight broke out over a petty theft, and he was clubbed to death on the beach by frenzied natives, within a few yards of his own armed crew.

After Captain Cook's death, King Kamehameha, whose dynasty eventually united all the islands, rose gradually to power. The old religion gradually lost its potency, leaving a vacuum into which flooded all the zeal of the first Congregational ministers from New England, who appeared in 1820, followed hotfoot by the Roman Catholics. The benefits bestowed by them upon the naked but innocent native are a source for conjecture, but at least hospitals and schools were established. Five King Kamehamehas came and went, the last dying without an heir in 1872, so thereafter the Hawaiian king was elected. The last two monarchs, Kalalaua and his sister Liliuokalani, tried to restore an absolute monarchy, and the succeeding upheaval ended in the annexation of Hawaii by the United States. Full statehood was granted in 1959, so now a fiftieth star twinkles on the American banner.

It is dusk by the time we are established in a charmless bedroom overlooking the car park. The terrace is illuminated by flickering torches and a luau, or Hawaiian feast, is in progress, complete with Polynesian food and hula dancing. Contrary to their reputation, these traditional dances express in mime, to the accompaniment of side-stepping bare feet and swaying hips, the cosmic piety of the Hawaiians and their veneration for the gods of nature. The dances, chants, and prayers are handed down through the generations and retain their purity through the exercise of the most rigorous discipline. Why does the word Hawaii, I wonder, instantly conjure up a vision of a salaciously swaying grass skirt, which, as a matter of interest, originated in the Gilbert Islands and not in Hawaii at all? Even the postman in Onslow Square entreated me to bring him back "one of them hula girls."

Morning light reveals the sun struggling successfully through a bank of cloud, so we thread a tortuous path seaward in search of "the play area." As the doors of the elevator open we seem at first glimpse to have emerged into an outsize day nursery. On all sides veterans in baby blue shorts and socks are competing against their consorts in pink rompers and diamanté goggles at table tennis, clock golf, shuffleboard, and quoits. On a travel-folder beach yet others are paddling, snorkling, and water-skiing. We hastily make for the uncluttered distance and slide into a sea like a blue caress, limpid and warm to the hand as a peach in the sun. As we wallow in it ecstatically (O frabjous day), a vision of Onslow Square, last seen under a cassock of snow, lurks before the inner eye.

Our hotel lies near the racy town of Lahaina, familiar to fans of James Michener's novel *Hawaii* as the center from which the royal house operated. Lahaina was once the whaling capital of the world, when lamps, stoves and torches everywhere were fed by whale oil, and the flexible bones of the baleen whale were highly prized for making corsets, bustles, and hoop skirts, as well as for buggy whips, fishing rods, and

111

riding crops. The whale is hunted to this day for its ambergris, the fixative for scent, a wax compound found in the intestine of an ailing sperm whale. The blubber is saved for cosmetics, soap, candles, and so forth, and huge iron cauldrons, originally used for rendering it down, still adorn the little town. Opposite the Pioneer Inn, the whalers' resort, was to be seen the *Carthaginian*, a square-rigged sailing bark, now, alas, at the bottom of the sea. With her sank a collection of relics and records of the 1840s when as many as five hundred whaling ships crowded into Lahaina every season.

The secretary of the Malacological Society of Hawaii has exhorted us to seek out a certain Mr. Charles King, conchologist, philosopher, and owner of a shell shop in Main Street. He towers monumentally behind a glass counter, perspiring lightly in an off-white singlet, sorting tiny shells with the dexterity of a jeweler.

"Take a dekko at these." A brilliant piebald cowry changes hands. "*Cypraea tesselata*. Worth $90 each. I'm packing 'em up for a museum. What? What? No, you'll never find 'em. My divers brought 'em in last week. No shells lying about on these beaches. You've gotta know where to go, and you gotta go with a boat and a skuba diver."

A beaded curtain behind him rattles and divides to admit an impassive Japanese girl with a face as still as carved ivory, who looks about thirteen, but who turns out to be twenty years old.

"My daughter," states Mr. King. "Adopted. Nothing about shells she don't know."

Mr. King's stock contains every known local shell, so that it is possible to take in the total range at a glance. His private collection is remarkable for its immense cowries. With some reluctance he parts with a gorgeous ivory one dappled with golden freckles measuring 122 mm. The immensity of this prize continues to rivet me until I display it on our return to members of the Conchological Society, one of whom owns one measuring 142 mm. This scholar disagrees with Mr. King's theory that the larger the cowries, the rarer they become, as if to protect themselves from the threat of extinction. They are large, he declares, because life is easy in tropical waters and, like you and me, a cowry puts on weight if it eats too much.

An inspection of Mr. King's triton shells turns the conversation to the scourge of starfish, the crown of thorns, already encountered in Fiji, and now decimating the coast of Guam and that of the Great Barrier Reef.

"It's bunkum," says Mr. King, "to say this pest is caused by

Starfish I have known. Crown of thorns, top left. Photograph by Sara Heaton.

over-collecting the tritons that prey on 'em. They hatch out or peg out with the changing temperature of the sea. A few degrees drop and the bastards die in the thousands and vice versa. Anyway, what else can you expect with all that blasting off on Bikini? And what about pollution? Proper mess they're making of the sea, and God knows where it'll end." Since it seems unlikely we shall encounter even a mussel on the shores of Maui, I pick out one of each species from his entire range for the eternal archives in Onslow Square.

Before taking to the water with a guide and the full equipment, we determine to explore the beaches beyond Kihei to the southwest. Pat has been warned that the springs of our Hertz car are uninsurable, and that we must under no circumstances leave the main road. Therefore, it is with caution that we edge our way along an earthy track, bouncing from one pothole to the next. It is not long before our rear wheels sink into the sand up to the axles. The tires spin like Catherine wheels giving off a reek of burning rubber. Since the nearest dwelling, a bird sanctuary, is at least fifteen miles back, we are probably here for life, so it seems prudent to examine the beach that will be our home, which we do at our leisure, enjoying a particularly pleasant bathe. Seaweed—purple, coral and black—lies in chic clusters on the foreshore. The customary husks of dead crayfish, lobsters, and crabs litter the sand, interspersed with splinters of coral. We do not spot a single shell. Returning to base, the car awaits us, an insolent smile on its radiator. We dig; we lay branches; we whirl the wheels, thus embedding ourselves more deeply; we push; we curse; we lay driftwood; we rock the chassis. Finally, Pat's good experience in extricating himself from snowdrifts in Buffalo prevails and, with a lurch and a hideous smell of sulphur, we are out.

Maui is shaped somewhat like an imperfect figure of eight, consisting of two mountainous masses joined at the waist by a low-lying plain. The northern portion, which contains Lahaina, supports two volcanoes, Eke and Puu Kukui, and the southern part the staggering Haleakala volcano, now dormant though not extinct, rising 10,000 feet sheer from beach level. Our attention is now drawn to remote beaches to the northeast, and still

We wind our way around the waist of Maui and up the ravine of Iao, where a spectacular monolith rises in verdant splendor 2,250 feet high from where we stand. Photograph by Patrick Hodgson.

hungering to find shells ourselves, perhaps with the aid of snorkling masks, we wind our way around the waist of Maui and up the ravine of Iao, where a spectacular monolith rises in verdant splendor 2,250 feet high from where we stand. Fabulous flowers, banks of blossoming vine and lush trees and shrubs cram every niche of the gorge, through which an exuberant stream falls in a series of glittering cascades. We strike the coast at a hamlet named Waihee, where cove after cove discloses itself with hardly a pebble, a piece of seaweed, or a shell upon it. Even snorkling over the rocks produces nothing. Pat spends twenty minutes chasing one black and white *Hastola hectica*, which is thrown up on the beach and sucked back by the undertow, eluding his grasp over and over again. If at first you don't succeed, you are not the eldest son.

As we are beating a frustrated retreat, the outline of the clapboard church, a slender steeple and a colonial-style vicarage, gives us pause. This must be Wailuku, the nerve center of the network of the original New England missionaries. For some reason we presume that like the Baldwin mission house in Lahaina it is open to visitors. A sonorous voice booms away behind the shutters and, assuming it to be that of a guide, we give the swing door a tentative push. It is immediately whipped open to its full extent. Framed in the doorway stands a vibrant figure.

"Come right in, folks!" he cries with a flash of gold teeth. "The feast is prepared!"

Smelling potently of brine and sun oil, we advance gingerly into an immaculate living room. Pat is in bathing shorts and I have bare feet.

"I think," we murmur, "that we have made a mistake. We thought this house was open to the public."

Mine eyes had seen the glory of a gleaming tea urn on a table covered with a lace cloth and laden with delicacies.

"Sure we are open to the public! Come on in and meet our good friends. After coffee I'm going to show you the joint myself. This is Mr. Chang, and this lady is Brigadier Ho li of the Salvation Army. And here are Mr. and Mrs. Zupnik of Wisconsin."

Mr. Zupnik, a majestic individual in braces, bows his acknowledgment. We introduce ourselves.

"And I am the Reverend Doctor Fay le Meadows, from Idaho. This is my wife, Meg. Where are you folks from?"

"London."

"London, O London! We just love that place, don't we Meg? We have our own little nest in the Kingsley Hotel, W.C. Meg and I just can't stay away from London, Mr. Hoskins, can we, Meg? Fifty-one straight plays and the best ballet in the world."

116

"Come right in, folks. . . . I am the Reverend Doctor Fay le Meadows, from Idaho."

Meg is a thin woman in her middle years, with perfectly dressed white hair through which is threaded a camellia. She is wearing excellent pearls and a lilac silk dress that falls to her silver sandals. Carrying a massive silver tray set with a stunning George II coffee set, she leads the way into a dining room lit by a candelabra of tapering white candles and by an illuminated black coral tree.

"Just help yourselves!" cries the truly hospitable doctor, extending fine hands with varnished nails rimmed in white, ornamented by a gold ring an inch wide and a golden bracelet.

"This cake is made from a Chinese recipe a thousand years old. Or this. It's octopus on sweet Portuguese bread. We brought the recipe from Lisboa. Lisboa's just fine, but it's Venice we like, don't we, Meg? We had a cute palazzo on the Grand Canal!"

We enquire about the denomination of the doctor's church, for the ambience is unfamiliar, and receive a somewhat evasive answer. He says he is an "outgrowth of the Congregational missionary thrust in 1823."

"You mean Abner Hale and Baldwin and the other chaps who came with the New England missions?"

(The student of *Hawaii*, who, unlike us, has read the preface, will already know that Abner Hale is a fictitious character, but we are still in the age of innocence and have been seeing him for days on every street corner.) The doctor seems to assent to this, but adds after a moment's thought, that "as more leadership was sent, the Wailuku Union Church was chartered."

"Oh, you mean yours in a Unionist church?"

"It is Congregational in background, affiliated with the United Church of Christ. We minister to all denominations." Well, this seems sensible in so polyglot a society, where it appears to reap a remarkable harvest, judging from the exotic group with whom we now move upstairs to examine the house.

"Here is *notre chambre*," announces our guide, ushering us into a dainty white bedroom decorated with pink rosebuds. "And we call our golden bathroom," opening the door to reveal the gilded splendor within, "the Lady Godiva bathroom."

Can these quarters be where they actually live, I wonder? No hairbrush, toothpaste, garment, book, crucifix, photograph, scent bottle, or spongebag mars the immaculate order of the rooms. Even the easel in the studio carries a blank white canvas, and on the side table waits an untouched palette, a fan of new paint brushes, and a box of unbroached tubes of paint. As we take our leave, stepping out of the candlelight into the sunshine, Doctor Fay le Meadows—I wonder how he fared in Idaho with a name like his?—hands me a signed sketch of himself. He is preaching from the rostrum illuminated by the dining room candelabra, while over his head he sports a halo. A momentary vision teases my memory—a shadow, a whisper of Liberace—and it is gone.

Torches are flaming, conch horns are blowing, and leis of roselana, a red cottage rose, are being cast upon the waters as a tribute to the demigod Maui when we return. It is the turn of our waiter, Hari, to make a ceremonial dive into the ocean as the sun sinks below the horizon, and his wink as he does so is very unceremonious indeed. Dolphin is dished up for dinner, tough as a rubber boot, described on the menu as *mahimahi.*

We are early afoot in Lahaina next morning to catch the first glass-bottomed boat to the reef and, we hope, to the reaches and beaches where breed the elusive shells of Maui. The boat lies rocking gently at anchor while a Chinese boy industriously polishes the brass, but there is no other sign of activity: "We go four o'clock." It is now nine fifteen. A pamphlet in our possession and also a prominent notice board advertises four daily sailings, at nine, twelve, two and four, adding enticingly: "Whales today."

"But aren't you going at noon?"

"Captain gone away. We go at four."

It is dazzlingly bright with the temperature already in the nineties, so we dive into the deeply shaded Baldwin Mission House, dated 1838, which Doctor le Meadows yesterday declared to be the home of the fictitious Abner and Jerusha Hale. The Reverend Dwight Baldwin became schoolmaster, doctor, dentist, justice of the peace, father of six children, and taught the Mauians to sing in harmony from this sturdy coral and stone house. Throughout his thirty-three violent years here, frenzied clashes occurred between the French, English, and American whalers, the heathen Mauians and the Puritan missionaries. We are dumbfounded to learn from a polyglot guide that Abner and Jerusha Hale existed only between the covers of *Hawaii* and in Mr. Michener's imagination. I haven't had a worse shock since I saw my brother Terry's boots protruding below Santa Claus's robe at a Christmas party when I was four. Our mentor shows us the original instructions issued by the American Board of Commissioners for Foreign Missions to Doctor Baldwin in 1820, which inform him that he is in the Sandwich Islands "for no private end, for no earthly object, but wholly for the good of others and for the Glory of God our Saviour." In these serene rooms, furnished with the possessions and tools of the good doctor's various vocations, is the simple affirmation of all the trust reposed in him.

From a shoreside eating house we watch three slate-colored humpback whales breaking water in Herculean leaps, each flaunting a double-pronged tail. Among them tawny youths are skimming shoreward, their surfboards balanced on the crest of convoluting rollers. Our beautiful young waitress, who makes Pat wish he were a whaler, has a sinister device tattooed on the inside of her forearm. Behind the bar a woman, her head tied in a violet silk scarf, seems to be in difficulties with the wreck of an obviously once presentable man. Under the balcony lollops our reef boat, heading for home, on which we can see the outline of the skipper at the wheel, looking not unlike a whale himself. As sailing time approaches, our progress towards the quay is stayed by a glimpse in Mike's Bar of a promising-looking aquarium, at the bottom of which strolls a cowry, unmistakably, *a Cypraea tesselata* in full fig, with extended foot and unfurled mantle ($90, dead or alive). We enter to examine it minutely. A frantic fish is darting to and fro, bashing its blunted nose against the sides of the tank. Mike leaves his bartending to peer with us anxiously into the depths.

"I doubt it that one is going to settle down. I reckon he don't like the baby moray eel—see, he's under this rock."

And so he is. Our old friend, having decided upon taking a bite, can't unlock his jaw even if he would.

We regain the waterfront in time to hear the reef boat omit one long bellow and see her go like a cow into her stall. The excursion to the reef demonstrates more lucidly than any words why we cannot find any shells. Below us lies a volcanic floor, decorated by an occasional rosette of grey coral but devoid of all else except blue water, an occasional school of wavering fish, the flap of a passing turtle, and, sometimes, the shadow of a basking shark.

"Sharks," remarks the skipper through the blower, "never attack here. The Hawaiians think it's because they're worshipped as gods of the sea. My guess is it's because the water's so warm there's plenty else for 'em to eat."

I join the captain at his wheel. He is pear-shaped, with a wiry beard and kinky black hair, springy as heather.

Only the Russians and the Japanese, he says, still take whaling seriously. They hunt with helicopters, shooting at them with missiles containing curare, which prevents them from breathing so they cannot submerge. By these means they kill as many as a hundred a day, previously the equivalent of a year's catch. At this rate they will be extinct in another two years.

For days we have been keeping a weather eye on the summit of Haleakala, our 10,032-foot home-grown volcano, which last erupted in 1750, an event heralded by a series of earthquakes. Haleakala means "house of the sun." Within it the demigod Maui once ensnared that heavenly body so that light perpetual might shine upon this island. Actually, clouds perpetual seem to envelope the peak, so the name is something of a misnomer. Today, however, the mountain justifies the labors of Maui by shining forth in its entirety. We bounce upward between bosomy foothills planted with pineapple, among bulls roving about in red fields, past a hippie singing to a guitar beside a stream.

The terrain rockets up 7,000 feet in 23 miles. The view suddenly disappears behind banks of scudding cloud as the kone wind springs up, the detested equivalent of the French mistral. With headlights now ablaze, we press on in bottom gear between boulders of lava covered in livid scrub. An occasional break in the cloud reveals the summit overlooking a crater seven miles wide. We scan the slope hopefully for the rapier-like leaves of the silversword plant, said to be peculiar to this particular mountain. It grows without flowering until just before it dies, when it explodes into a vivid purple and yellow flower. A cross between a cactus and a yucca, it is actually a member of the sunflower family but has remained unique through its evolution in so isolated a habitat. We do not need a warning posted on the way to walk slowly at this elevation, for our hearts are thumping and our ears cracking before we start the final climb to the summit. Once there, however, the whole thing closes up into one comprehensible whole. Pele, Maui, Kane, Ku, Kaneloa, Leno, and the Immortals; the sky, the sea, the wind, the volcano, and the hula dancers. It all makes sense.

"Do you know what scrimshaw is?"
"Yes"
"What is it?"

"Let's think. A scrimshaw is—er—someone who doesn't do his share of the chores."

"Wrong. It's a sort of etching done by sailors on whalebone."

Now we have scrimshaw in our shell museum.

Other people find shells. Why can't we? The locals under-standably prefer to get them themselves and sell them to us, but even so there must be divers with boats, who exist but for hire and reward, so why not our reward? Pat is soon to be seen in conference with a nautical figure leaning against the bar in the Pioneer Inn. You might suppose this inn to have been too publicized by the film *Hawaii* to keep it's authentic flavor, but this is not so. The swinging doors into the saloon bar, the whaling tackle rusting on the wall, the huge brass spittoons, the stuffed fish, the blackened cauldrons, and a row of iron torches have remained unchanged for over a hundred years. The saloon is crammed with sailors, including a drunk reciting *Hiawatha* with·a Harvard accent.

We are not much impressed at first with Harold Hale when Pat brings him over to our table, for he is agonizingly shy. We gather, however, that he owns a boat, aqualungs, diving gear, and has local knowledge; and once he is hired, Harold comes to life. Why, we ask him, can't we corner so much as a peri-winkle? The answer seems to be that in 1946 and again in 1960 huge tidal waves hit Maui, in each of which, incidentally, Harold lost a boat. I've always pictured such a wave to be a towering wall of water with a vast curling crest, like the Hokusai wood-cut of the Manazawa wave, but Harold says it's not like that at all. A tidal wave is preceded by a terrific suck back, like an immensely low tide, which grounds all the boats and maroons thousands of fish and turtles, which flap about in the pools. Then a great cliff of water rushes forward, advancing at a terrifying speed, followed by about seven lesser surges, lasting in all between four and five hours. In both these disasters hun-dreds of Mauians were drowned while dragging the shallows for fish, and all the small craft were smashed. Water also inundated the low-lying land, depositing thousands of fabulous shells on all the beaches and mudbanks. Harold seized the chance to form a big collection, but the rich vein, he says, is now exhausted.

Tidal waves originate in submarine earthquakes. With modern methods of measuring them, the population now gets a previous warning. Everyone on land withdraws up into the hills while all the boats rush out to meet and to be borne up on the wave, which, having no crest, is hardly perceptible at sea. In Japan for instance, in 1896, a wave devastated the island of Honsho. Fishermen at sea noticed nothing unusual until they put in to port, there to be met by scenes of desolation and a death roll of 27,000.

When Harold was seventeen, he was out skuba diving one morning and suddenly remembered a date with a girl friend. As happens sometimes when sailors are escaping from a submarine, he surfaced too fast. As a result he nearly died of an acute attack of the bends, which left him permanently crippled. Since then he has earned his poi by renting his boat, by a limited amount of cautious diving, and by fishing for turtle. He says the most valuable part of the turtle is the cilipe, a cartilaginous substance that holds the breastbone together and endows the soup with that succulent chunk of greenish meat.

We get up to go. "I'm sure being careful today!" says Harold bleakly. "Three days ago two of my best friends went out diving and never came back. Nobody knows what happened. We just found the empty boat."

Outside, the inevitable kone has sprung up and is blowing in all directions at once, while whitecaps hiss across the bay. We all get drenched—all, that is to say, except Harold who is hermetically sealed into a diving suit. The freak storm has stirred up the sand for half a mile out from the shore. Visibility below the surface is therefore nil, so Harold is unable to see his hand before his face, even if he should wish to do so. So, as usual, no shells today.

"I'm fed up to the back teeth with shelling."
"I am too."
"I don't care if I never see another shell."
"You never will if we stay here much longer."

"Let's go down to the play center, or whatever they call it, and have a game of clock golf."

No sooner are we established in bloated comfort beside the pool, sheltered by a beach umbrella, with tinkling drinks on an occasional table, when Bernard Nuuhiwa, the beachboy, materializes before us. He carries a sort of toasting fork made from a wire coat hanger, and his face is crumpled with concern.

"I saw Harold in Mike's Bar! He say you find no single shell, not one, on the Island of Maui."

We agree this is so.

"But many shells in front of hotel! By this rock fishermen clean their catch. Here! Throw guts in the sea, so! Many cowries, many cones, many moray eels; all come to feed here." The fork is proffered as if it were the town mace.

"Now! You do like me. You put on mask. You float face down over rocks in two foot of water, not moving, see? Cowries hidden under rocks, in holes, under sea urchins. Do not splash with water. Nor put hand in hole because of moray eels. Rake 'em out with fork, so!"

Pat is up and into the water before you could say *Tympanotonus radula*. I follow keenly and, in my haste, as it turns out, break the little toe on my right foot and am unable to wear a shoe for six weeks.

This approach produces a small black serpent's head cowry, a Hebrew cone, and a medium-sized auger. A crock of gold could hardly be more rewarding. Bernard is standing up to his knees in water, watching us anxiously. To encourage us, he has rushed home to fetch his own catch from this reef, which includes a blond leopard cone covered in orderly black spots; several dark reticulated cowries, all of a good size; some Isabel's cowries dappled in fawn, about an inch in length; a number of gold ring cowries, and a plethora of augers in mixed sizes and shades. And tomorrow we move to Hana on the other side of the island!

During the night all four tires of our Hertz car are deflated by some loving hand. The road, when belatedly we merge into it, follows the foothills of the volcano Haleakala down to the shore, then swerves inland into the mountains. The conical hills are threaded with torrential streams that cascade into pools whose banks are smothered in brilliant savage flora. Trees aspire to bewildering heights, vines loop downward and trail in dazzling convolutions of color, scent, and shape. Orange cliffs fall sheer, thousands of feet to a cerulean sea, which crashes into weirdly formed coves and caves. The road writhes upward and further upward, with Pat driving more often than not with one wheel in the ditch to avoid the light-hearted traffic coasting down. This affords an opportunity to observe the hedgerows at close range; they are rife with botanical strangers. Overlooking a gorge, deserted except for wheeling white birds, stands an oriental temple, its double door thrown invitingly open. Removing our sandals, we approach a golden image with lowered lids and an archaic smile, before which are piled votive offerings of rice, water, and roses. Mortal and immortal, we exchange a long, considering gaze, neither side revealing any clue to the other.

The last thirty miles to Hana Ranch takes two hours of tightly packed hairpin-bend driving. Gradually the country opens out into lush meadows, thronged with wild horses and hundreds of Hereford cattle. This was originally a pineapple-growing area until a Mr. Paul Fagan built a ranch, putting the land down to pasture. When he realized how many islanders were in consequence thrown out of work, he turned his ranch into a hotel, adding wings of modern cottages and employing only Mauian labor.

A doe-eyed girl greets us with frosted glasses of passion-fruit juice. Our cottage is furnished with considerable taste and overlooks the sea and some hazy hills. On each pillow reposes a scarlet hibiscus, while in the washbasin floats a drift of ginger flowers. A cocktail party by the poolside is in progress, to which we are bidden, an experience that calls to mind the initial day of the first term at school. Everybody seems to know everyone else intimately, as indeed they do, since Hana is a meeting place for habitués. The creases have not yet hung out of our clothes, and, owing to my broken toe, I am barefoot. Surely none of these glamorous strangers will cast more than a passing glance at us, crumpled misfits that we are, so we stay ourselves with rum and comfort ouselves with foie gras. It there-

125

fore comes as an agreeable surprise to be accosted by the most striking couple in sight, Bruce and Jackie Anderson. A lofty man of considerable presence, Bruce has a straight hazel gaze and smiling lines lift up the corners of both eyes and mouth, while Jackie looks like a heroine in some Edwardian novel. She is golden and white and blue in all the right places, with a smile like a benediction. Whenever they can escape from Texas, they rush down to Hana. They have bought a headland on which they hope eventually to build, but in the meantime they keep a stable and a boat here. Their main interest is in the ancient art and culture of the islands.

Every night since arriving in Maui we have watched some form or other of hula dancing, of which I have been a narrow observer. Slowly it becomes apparent that each gesture is of precise significance. In a subtle deaf and dumb alphabet, messages are being spelt out by supple and delicate hands, synchronized with gliding steps and swinging hips. Once you get the hang of it, it's no harder than reading semaphore. Thus when early morning brings forth the opportunity of a hula lesson with a circular Mauian lady, Josephine, I am at the starting tape in the Calabash Suite sharp at the appointed hour. The rudiments, the basic movements, and the reason for the dance are demonstrated to the class by Josephine, who, for all her bulk, is as light on her feet as a bubble and pulsating with rhythm.

> "It's not the island fair that is calling to me,
> Not the balmy air, not the tropical sea . . ."

She sings, her feet flying, arms undulating, hips working like an eggbeater. A trickle of water outside accompanies her, running discreetly down, a muted scale like the sweep of fingers across a harp. No one in the class will ever see fifty again, and all are hampered by a heavy breakfast of recent memory, yet such is her magnetism that her inept pupils are soon aloha-ing on the close-carpeting as if they were on the moonlit strand at Waikiki.

A cook-in around the pool that evening terminates in a Hawaiian entertainment, if that is the word; it is inaudible,

Josephine, mistress of the hula, who, for all her bulk, is as light on her feet as a bubble. Maui, Hawaii. Photograph by Patrick Hodgson.

A trickle of water outside accompanies her, running directly down a muted scale like the sweep of fingers across a harp. Maui, Hawaii. Photograph by Martha Hodgson.

lengthy, and underrehearsed. Crowned and festooned in rosalas, Josephine floats by like a captive balloon.

"*My* class," she hisses in passing, "can do better than this!"

Breakfast is planned on the beach at sunrise, and pilgrims who have followed this narrative until now will not be surprised to hear that Pat and I oversleep. Strangers in these parts, we cannot find the cliff path. We wander the fields among the fecundity of the Herefords, all of whom have one or more calves, until we spot the dazzling Jackie Anderson sprinting down a gully, a calabash held before her as in the egg and spoon race.

"Are you chasing something?"

"No. I just feel like running."

"Running anywhere special?" (Perhaps she is running towards breakfast.)

"There is a fresh water spring behind those rocks."

Well that's a start anyway. The water is sweet and cold and tastes of calabash. Those who have arrived on horseback have tethered the horses in a grove close by and, hidden from view beyond some rocks, the barbecue is in full spate. (Steaks, sausages, mushrooms, eggs, bacon, corn bread, pineapple, papaya, peaches, and coffee.) Last night Pat and I examined one another's waxing waistlines with mutually uncomplimentary comments. From now on we resolved to eat a continental breakfast only. I remind Pat of this decision as he broaches a steak.

"Yes indeed," he replies after some self-communion, "but the question is which continent?"

Below the rocks is a beach where a turbulent arrangement of water advances in giant rollers. It breaks, rearranges itself, breaks again, and dashes up the beach with much displacement of notably gritty sand. Here Pat girds himself for an expedition to an emerging reef as if for a crusade, with helmet, huge gloves, and a long sword shaped like a meat skewer.

"Come on," he says bracingly, wading into the boiling surf.

I say I am afraid.

"Afraid? What of? I mean of what?"

"I am afraid of those waves."

"Nonsense. All you have to do is to dive through them."

And do you know he is perfectly right? The most exhilarating bathe ensues, during which Pat nearly bursts a lung diving for an exotic object gleaming on the reef; it turns out to be a bottle top.

The Andersons are in the bar drinking rum within a circle of locals when we return to the ranch, and the word "shells" floats towards us on the fumes. Among them is a horticulturist, Howard Cooper, who raises amaryllis on a large scale. He lifts his voice to complain that while we are scrambling about in search of marine mollusks, he has the reverse problem, there being a plague of land snails, which weigh up to half a pound each, the *Achatina fulica*, from Africa. It seems that they were imported by a Japanese farmer to serve up as a dainty dish to his ducks, who are passionately addicted to them. To restabilize the balance, a cannibal shell from the Caribbean has been introduced, the *Euglandina rosea*, a smaller snail, which is now busily devouring the greater. It can be seen from time to time perched upon its prey, enjoying a leisurely luncheon. The day will eventually dawn, hopes poor Mr. Cooper, whose entire crop has been devoured, when the cannibals, having polished off the *Achatina fulica*, will start on one another.

"You know it is a remarkable thing," puts in another resident, John Elliot, "that at night you can hear them singing."

"Snails singing? How do you mean? Tosti's 'Goodbye' and all that?"

"Well, the bastards sort of—er—HUM."

Mr. Elliot is engaged in building himself a house in the neighborhood, an enterprise proving to be less of a lark than he had anticipated. Not only has it been necessary to import the entire house, built in San Francisco and broken down into numbered parts, but he has also had to bring in carpenters to erect it, and to pay for their keep. It is conveyed to the party in an undertone by Jackie Anderson that this will be a house to out-house all houses. A few days later, while searching for the Seven Sacred Pools, we come across this retreat, nobly sited on a headland and appointed with such basic necessities as an aviary, an orchid house, and a Roman swimming pool.

Howard Cooper enquires how we clean our shells once we have found them. Like a Greek chorus, Pat and I bewail the hideous penultimate day of every holiday spent in bathrooms from the Scillies to Singapore, all unavailingly, as it happens, since autumn is always far advanced before the shells of spring are finally purged.

"How would it be," asks Mr. Cooper, after some moments of silent brooding, "if you dissolved the creature in its shell? Just a few drops of papaya juice—green, not ripe, mark you—have the effect of reducing protein into liquid. Why wouldn't it work?" Pat protests that a green papaya tree does not grow in every back garden.

"Then try Adolph's Meat Tenderizer—plain. Its reaction on meat is exactly the same. If you put on enough you ought to be able to pour the guy out of his shell."

What a pity that, almost for the first time in our lives, we haven't got a dead mollusk between us.

Meanwhile, preparations for a great feast, a *lu'aa*, are in progress on the beach. Tiki, the gardener, is plaiting palm fronds into rakish hats, while his brother is busy raising a timber platform. Two chefs have already dug an eight-foot pit, lit a log fire at the base, and on it have piled stones that will eventually become red hot. Upon these a pig is destined to be roasted whole.

When the pig arrives, he is seen to be trussed and split down the middle, his sightless eyes glaring, his snout turned convulsively upward, looking for all the world like some luckless missionary being served up at a Fijian beano. His innards are first sprinkled with sea salt, then red-hot stones are placed in key positions in the carcass, which immediately ignites, giving off a heady aroma. It was a similar whiff from some pig, accidentally cooked alive, which suggested to the ancient Chinese that there are better ways of enjoying pork than eating it raw. Lastly, the pig is lowered upon the smoking ti leaves, which have been moistened with seawater from a sacramental-looking vessel. The pit is then filled up with sand. The pig weighs 118 pounds and will take four hours to cook.

At dusk, crowned in leaves and leis, the guests arrive to watch their dinner being eased out of the pit by a team of sweating cooks. A limb or two drops off into the fire and is retrieved.

Lastly, the pig is lowered upon the smoking ti leaves. Maui, Hawaii.
Photograph by Patrick Hodgson.

Rum punch is served from a cauldron to everyone, including
the staff who, their aims accomplished, fling themselves whole-
heartedly into the pursuit of happiness. Torches are lit, conches
are blown. Flowers are scattered upon the tables. The chef's
two daughters and his niece, plus our chambermaid, Maria,
take up their stance on the creaking platform, swaying and
pulsing with song. Warbling waitresses dish out gargantuan
portions of pig. Bruce and Jackie are on intimate terms with
each laden platter-bearer, and soon our plates too contain not
only pig, but chicken, mahimahi, rice, sweet potato, shrimps,
and the staff of life, poi, in extra measure. A carton of this key
nourishment is set before each guest, many of whom eye it
with reserve. In Maui a man must earn his poi, but do we,
having done nothing to deserve it, actually have to eat it? In

131

appearance it resembles wallpaper paste and in taste a wash-cloth. Yet it takes much labor to produce, for the taro root must be gathered, winnowed, and pounded with pestle and mortar, followed by long cookings and stirrings. It seems churlish to refuse nourishment upon which so many hours of loving manpower have been lavished. However, all the more for the Mauis who, with delighted faces, are soon spooning it down in the cookhouse.

Josephine, mistress of the hula, is now to be seen undulating upon the platform, from which she beckons Pat to join her. With flying sulu (his Fijian skirt), a swinging lei of nuts, and a pineapple balanced on his head, he joins in with such abandon that, amid hilarious applause, Tony de Jetley, the manager, crowns him with a headdress woven from palm fronds. After this Pat nearly pokes out my eye with a spike each time he turns his head, which is often, for he is wearing a ginger flower behind his ear in the "I am available" position.

Back at the ranch Pat, still crowned in spikes, engages me in a desperate battle of checkers. Bruce, whom I regret to report has drunk too much rum, puts me off my game by narrating his personal saga into my ear in so compelling a manner that Pat huffs me off the board three times running. Oil slumps; fortunes disappear overnight; brains are blown out; geysers ignite; new strikes are made. The mind reels.

"I have come up, if up I am, the hard way. Jackie is the only one who's any good in our family," continues Bruce inexorably.

"Huff you."

"Damn, I didn't see it."

"Yup, I'm just an old reprobate. A glutton. A boozer. And I talk too much. And do you know something else?" Dramatic pause. "Sometimes I spit!"

"Huff you."

Pat's sulu is somewhat doubtfully received among some of the unversed American males. Is he a queer, perhaps, or a hippie, of which there are plenty here, or just a transvestite? The Mauian girls, however, nurture no such doubts, and from this night forth Pat has but to lift a little finger for service, while I bask in his reflected glory.

Rumors describing the unsurpassed beauty of the Seven Pools, sacred to the goddess Pele, into which no mortal dares to plunge, are circulated by the car hire brethren. It is at some inconvenience that we hairpin along the coast to case these pools, which turn out to be set in dismal ice-cold volcanic ravines where no sane mortal would bathe anyway. A Mrs. May, from Upper Slaughter in the Cotswolds, with her Hawaiian husband, both in swimsuits, are examining the water with contempt.

"I think we'll go back and bathe at the hotel," is their sensible verdict. Mrs. May turns out to be an expert on dressage who was invited to Oahu to train an Olympic equestrian team. In the Sea-Life Park at this time was a recalcitrant whale who could neither eat nor sleep and who bit everyone who approached her, so in despair her keeper called in Mrs. May to tame her. Celestine, for such is the whale's name, is now a prima donna, leading exponent, perhaps, of the dance of the seven whales.

Oil has slumped again and the Andersons have been recalled to Texas. As a farewell gesture Bruce sends us a bowl of leonine orchids that, in the interests of safety, is temporarily placed on the floor. When the telephone rings I catapult out of the bathroom, step in the bowl and pitch on to the bed.

"Hello?"

"I'm just ringing up to say goodbye."

"Goodbye."

"Anything the matter?"

"I've just trodden in the bowl of orchids."

"My dear Martha, what a glamorous misadventure!"

We are now so completely at home that we might have been in Maui for years. The dancers who go on tonight are the hired help, now all old friends, and what they lack in slickness they make up for in verve, grace, and a sense of fun. After the show, from which they recuperate with drafts of Budweiser on the house, I sit among them as if in a cage of parakeets. Only one is a stranger, this being her first day out of hospital. She drops down beside me with a swish of skirts, leis, and streaming black hair.

"Once I was in London."

"Did you enjoy yourself there?"

"Yes, but no fog. Very dull. Just sun, like here. I want to see a pea-souper."

"We don't have them any more."

"No! Not? In London I stay in Piccadilly Square. I visit that prison where they chopped off the wahine's (women's) heads. Very fine there, with all the Queen's crowns. And many soldiers, guarding. Very good, in high-buzz hats." Gesture. "You know my friend Helen? Not? She marry manager of Paladium Theater. When I go there I sit in Queen's chair." (I, too, once sat in Queen's chair in Royal Box. Show opened with National Anthem and where were grandchildren? On floor fighting like dervishes over a penny.)

"I give you Helen's number. You call her when you get to London. Yes?"

Actually, no.

It has now become an accepted fact that, short of a convenient tidal wave before our departure for Oahu tomorrow, no shells are likely to pass into our possession except over a shop counter. Our mood is despondent but resigned. It is suddenly modified, however, by the appearance of Josephine, her muumuu kilted to the knee, armed with a crook and a basket.

"No one tell me you want shells! I know beaches where plenty shells."

"You do? How far?"

The crook indicates a series of coves immediately below the hotel, and remembering the lesson of Bernard at Kaanapali, we follow her meekly along a flowering hedgerow through some hundreds of Hereford cattle towards the sea. It is disturbing among so much uniformity to see several milk white Charelois and coal black Angus unconcernedly stuffing themselves, unaware, poor things, that they are odd cow out. They must be color blind.

Josephine is amused at our concern. "*Hoomanawanui* (Take it easy)," she suggests soothingly, a phrase often upon Mauian lips. Splendid Jack Lines, she explains, overseer of the 40,000 head on this ranch, and husband to Daisy behind the bar, is cautiously inaugurating a new strain through these very intruders, who are already in calf.

After a couple of hours of strenuous beachcombing upon a flinty red sand beach, the total catch is a few beaten up cones, two dead cowries and some cannibal snails. The cold comfort of the harvest is offset for Pat and me, however, by our interest in watching a strange creature anchored at the base of a rocky pool. Its white tentacles a yard or so long, like undulating spaghetti, creep into crevices, encircle tiny plants, and delicately probe beneath pebbles for prey.

En route for Honolulu the next morning, we pass within sight of Pearl Harbor. In an attack upon the Japanese, Pat once sailed from here in an aircraft carrier on which he sustained his only war wound.

"I didn't know you were ever wounded."

"Indeed I was, wearing silk pyjamas too. I put my head out of the porthole of the captain's cabin just as they fired off a gun."

"Good gracious! What happened?"

"My eyelashes were blown off."

Our objective is Waikiki Beach, in spite of ghoulish reports of the "billion dollar building boom." Perhaps this lovely beach has suffered more than anywhere else in Oahu in the seven years since we last saw it, for it has practically disappeared under a relentless tide of high-rise buildings. Even Diamond Head is not immune. Skyscrapers mar its lower slopes, and as we fly over the crater of the volcano we see them going up even inside. But who will laugh last if it ever erupts?

Nothing, however, can destroy the splendor of the bay itself, where the long lazy rollers follow one another slowly landwards, crashing endlessly down on the moon white sand. Crouching on their heavy boards, sometimes accompanied by an incoming yacht or a native outrigger hewn from a tree trunk, the surfers come flying shoreward on the towering crests. It is the latter craft that engage our fascinated attention, and it is not long before we are established in one of them. Pat is placed in the bow position with me immediately behind him. Hyppolyte and Mink, the owners, both clad unfussily in a single wisp of flame cotton, sit one behind the other in the stern. We paddle evenly out to sea, riding straight through the incoming surf. Beyond the line of breakers we turn and manoeuvre for position, awaiting the advent of a real whopper, which occurs about once in every ten waves. It forms; it advances; it towers. The outrigger swings its tail towards the advancing breaker.

"Paddle!" yells Hyppolyte from the stern, and we obey like crazy.

The wave lifts us upon its boiling crest, and we are flying like sea gulls through rainbows of spray. Other frenziedly paddling figures also rise through the foam to the summit of the wave. Abreast we skim towards shore, collapsing together in the broken water, surfers, boards, canoes, and paddles, amid ribaldry and yells of triumph. Time and time again we all struggle up through the surf, collect our gear and until the sun goes down head out to sea again and again for more.

On the morning that we leave we find the airport in gala mood, for the new Pan Am 747 has just made her maiden landing and is standing up to her ankles in a mob of carefree admirers. So normal is she in proportion that until seen up against some lesser aircraft she looks like any other hummingbird. No sooner has the turbulence of her departure subsided when a sleek navy blue and white VC10, en route for Australia, deposits the Queen, the Duke, Princess Anne, and a retinue of forty-five upon the red carpet just vacated by the jet set. They emerge from the aircraft to a hurricane of song from a girl's choir clad in ankle-length white muumuus, and a clash of arms from the Guard of Honor dressed in the deep blue and white uniforms of the Royal Guards of the late King Kamahameha. All three stand blithely in the sunshine, loaded with ceremonial leis and surrounded by singers, soldiers, VIPs, garlands, and flags.

Presently, headed in the opposite direction, we are established in two port seats of a 707 while, in the equivalent seats to starboard, sit two men of vaguely familiar appearance. The nearer of the two, a disciple of the principle of togetherness, instantly introduces himself as Mr. Earl Thacker of Hana, Honolulu, and somewhere in Texas. After some, but not much, conversation he gives us a photograph of his grandchildren, duly autographed. We thank him. He invites us to visit him in Texas and adds his address to the photograph. We thank him again. He introduces his friend, whose name we do not catch but who, after one horrified glance, disappears behind the *Wall Street Journal*. Mr. Thacker announces he will now join the captain in the cockpit, and pads silently off in pale blue socks. His friend lowers his newspaper and looks keenly down at Maui over which we are flying. We point out landmarks to one another and he smilingly says he is building a house at Kipahulu, near Hana, indicating the spot. It was from the air, he adds, that he first became aware of the need to preserve the environment and of the full extent of the destruction taking place. I ask him if he flies around much, to which he replies, "a certain amount." He has just succeeded, he confides, in getting a measure passed to conserve the blue and the humpback whale for which, we learn later from Mr. Thacker, he has been awarded the Bernard Baruch prize. Both men are trying to push through a development program to protect Maui before it is too late.

"Pity they didn't slap down conservation orders on Waikiki Beach and Diamond Head before they mucked them up with those eyesores," remarks Pat.

"Eyesores?" barks Mr. Thacker. "I happen to live in one of them." The conversation switches hastily to shells and we describe our experiences, or lack of them, in Maui. Mr. Thacker turns towards his friend:

"Wasn't your wife's book about shells—*A Gift from the Sea*"—a best seller?"

"*Gift from the Sea?*" I repeat. "By Anne Lindbergh? It's been my favorite book for years."

Mr. Thacker's friend was General Charles Lindbergh, no less, the "Lone Eagle," the world's hero and mine, who, in 1927, flew a single-engined plane, *The Spirit of St. Louis*, solo across the Atlantic.

Although his wife, Anne, wrote this engaging book years before the birth of my obsession for shells, every word of it, except for the title, struck an answering chord. For I have found the sea to be an unpredictable donor, one whose gifts can be extracted from it only with blood, mud, stings, septic scratches, and a broken toe.

In the meantime I flashed a look of startled recognition at the general. He and his wife were known to live in Darien a life of almost total seclusion. But his observant untroubled eyes remained unguarded. For a few seconds we looked straight at one another, each reading, as it were, the small print at the back of the other's eyes. In mine he would have seen involuntary homage. In his I saw the chart of a fine intellect, of quiet strength, and a spirit both intuitive and gentle.

The plane started to pitch and the general disappeared into the cockpit, Mr. Thacker divulged that "Slim" Lindbergh was one of the test pilots for the new 747. (It was later reported on the radio that we were groping our way in between tornados and waterspouts.) Nevertheless we floated in like a bubble and the rumor was that it was the hand of the general who deposited us so gently upon the runway.

As it turned out, the Eagle completed his unassuming house near Hana just in time, to fold his wings there forever, and to be received into the rust-red earth of Kipahulu's little graveyard.

Pat and I have now reached the parting of our ways. Tomorrow he flies westward to London, I south to Sarasota to stay with my brother, H.H.H. Munro, known on three continents as Hurry Hurry Hurry, but to you and me less formally as "Terry."

7 Siesta Key, Sanibel, Captiva

With red hair, a monocle, and the power to command the respectful attention of headwaiters in several capital cities and elsewhere, as a young man my brother was a captivating companion. *En secondes noces* he married a southerner, Gladys Arnold, known as "G." Whenever I try to describe her, Robert Louis Stevenson's rather overcharged verses addressed to His Mate appear automatically on the screen of my inner eye. I can therefore do no less than quote one line: "Trusty, dusky, vivid, true."

The onset of Parkinson's disease forced Terry into early retirement, and his body has become progressively enslaved to this baffling illness—but not, however, his spirit. He and G have fought it every inch of the way. Despite desperate trials, the twinkle has never entirely left Terry's eye; it seems only to have become more pronounced. A neighbor of theirs in Siesta Key, in the same predicament and under a similar regime, made a startling recovery. It is, he says, as if he had stepped out of a suit of steel armor. The generous delight shown to him by the stricken Munros is profoundly touching.

Terry's house is a low, comfortable, clapboard affair with French windows open towards the sea on the one hand, and on the other overlooking a lagoon leaping with fish, a rendezvous for birds and dragonflies. Inside, Georgian furniture is sedately placed against uncluttered pale buff walls. A water green petit point carpet, consisting of twelve closely observed shell designs ordered by G from the Royal School of Needlework, was, as you might expect, completed in record time. The most insensible visitor will instinctively skirt this sensational carpet, setting his cloddish feet anywhere rather than upon it.

Unable to sleep on the first night I slip through a long window into the garden and hover barefoot on the verge of the lagoon. The moon is almost full, a near-perfect orb, reflected in the glass-bright black water. Outlandish patterns of leaf, fruit, and flower cast lace shadows on the silvered grass.

> Adorned with yellow pears
> And with wild roses filled
> The earth hangs in the lake.

The night and I are face to face, as it were, for the first time, and for some reason my eyes prick with sudden tears. Misted over prismatically, I might be looking at some hazy gouache painted by Monet or Cézanne. Maybe the vision of painters such as these was all too often seen through a mist of tears.

Siesta Key is a flat sandy island a few miles south of Sarasota, on the fringe of a shell belt that includes also the superb beaches of Sanibel, Captiva, and Marco, as well as some ten thousand other islands, which lie north of the Everglades swampland. When Pat first came to these parts on fishing trips, the population, particularly of his favorite Marco, consisted mainly of poor whites and Indians, who made a living by hunting in winter and fishing in spring. But now every March a great shell fair takes place on Sanibel Island, which, from humble beginnings in the porch of the old Island Inn, has developed into an international conchological event. Collectors descend upon it from all over the world both to exhibit and to gloat over the treasures of others, which are assembled in the Community House built for the purpose. The exhibition is open now, and an immediate expedition is planned.

The route lies down the Tamiami Trail, which unrolls before us in a dead straight line like a white hot ribbon. Ten years ago the landscape consisted of a perfect circle of sawgrass and swamp, level as the ocean, unbroken by hill or tree.

Now its Attic simplicity is scarred by shantytowns, caravans, petrol pumps, and billboards, interspersed by clumps of balding pines. A bridge and a bird-haunted causeway have replaced a ferry as a link between the mainland and Sanibel. The glory of this island, which is waist-high in desultory scrub, lies in its beaches of ivory sand that shelve gradually out into the Gulf of Mexico. Impelled by low, warm waves, the shells roll gently in and lie, waiting to be garnered like flowers, rose pink, nasturtium, lilac, and primrose; mottled, freckled, striped, and pearly. Occasionally, a violet snail or a paper nautilus rides in on the convolution of a wave and alights like a bubble on the sand. This is the very shore dreamed of and prayed for on the slug-and-serpent-ridden reefs of Pacifica.

Terry is established in the shade with the *Wall Street Journal*, looking like an elder statesman in a panama hat and monocle, while G and I succumb to the shimmering magic around us. There are literally thousands of shells, some piled in luminous drifts, others scattered prodigally over the glittering shore. The problem is where to start. The most soothing technique is to stretch out beside a mound of shells and to sift slowly through it. This is the method I choose, while my whole being is aware of the singing sun on my back, the piping of the warblers and egrets, the purling of the waves, and the texture and complexion of the shells as they slip through my fingers. G adopts the alternative system. Bent double, with eyes intent, she zigzags off and soon is swallowed up by distance. An hour or two glides by before we recall the object of the enterprise, the shell fair. Here we find world-wide collections of a staggering variety. The "shell of the year" is a four-inch lavender-hued cone from Taiwan, the *Conus kinoshitai*. The prize-winning local shell, found only the evening before the opening, is a huge albino, like white porcelain, a *Pleuroplaca reevei*. Humbler exhibits include dozens of variations of one specimen and growth series that show a shell at every stage from egghood to maturity. The live marine tank, however, is best of all. In it shells, fish, starfish, crabs, and eels are shacked up together apparently on amicable terms, resulting no doubt from digestive peculiarities that make them averse to eating each other.

141

Needless to say, no detail of an exhibition of shell pictures, escapes me. When you consider the limitations of the medium, the variety is surprising. It is, for example, almost impossible to produce a straight line. Ideas and emotions may surge up within the artist's breast, but the problem is how to express them from such intractable material. My own view is that the most successful pictures are those in which the artist has forgotten himself and has conceived some simple design that lets the ravishing beauty of the shells speak for themselves. Apparently that great jeweler, Richard Morrell, of Collingwood's in London, endorsed this view. Bemused by a small brown shell that emerged from Pat's pocket, the pearl Trigonia, he once remarked:

"Not I, nor any of my craftsmen, can create anything so exquisite as the unthinking mollusk."

Garlands of flowers made from shells, displays of sea freaks, of marine fossils, of agatized coral, and elaborate arrangements

"Not I, nor any of my craftsmen," said the jeweler, "can create anything so exquisite as the unthinking mollusk." The pearl trigonia (*Neotrigonia margaritacea* Lamarck). Photograph by Sara Heaton.

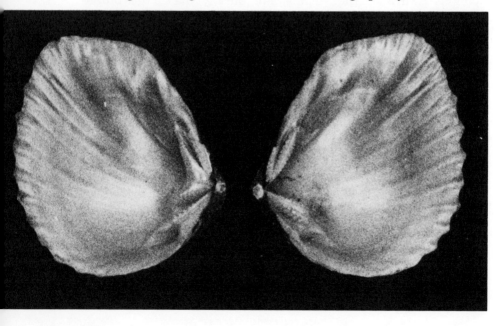

of driftwood produce a trancelike atmosphere, as if one were living at the bottom of an aquarium. So an antidote is welcome in the form of a Vesuvian hot dog stand. At this sizzling rendezvous I find the owner of the shell shop in Maui, Mr. King, and his equivalent from the Cayman Islands, Sid, last seen on Christmas Day in his native Georgetown trying to sell us a basket of extremely high—and I don't mean tall—helmet shells.

The old-timers at the stall seem a bit nonplussed by the whole turn of events. They reminisce nostalgically about the Island Inn—once a simple affair of rough cottages clustered round a dilapidated central block, each with a tap, bucket, and bench where the shellers could clean their catch and a nest of tables on which to display it. Towards the end of the season each of the two hotels gave its own show, displaying treasure that all had had an equal chance to find, but which had gone to the earliest riser or the sharpest eye. There used to be a glass case in the lobby of the inn where the rarities among Sanibel shells were put on show, and the whole island tingled with excitement each time a junonia or a lemon pecten came to light. Then again, a shell as rare as mimosa in Iceland during one season would proliferate upon the beach in the next, and vice versa. What next? You never knew. Now everything's up to date on the island and they have even built a high-rise condominium on the shore. No, the good old days will never come back to Sanibel, but the shells ride in uncaring, while overhead shine the everlasting stars.

Sanibel and its sister island, Captiva, lie a few miles off the West Florida coast in San Carlos Bay. Once the haunt of the Caloosa Indians, they were captured by the Spaniards in the sixteenth century by Ponce de Leon, who named the island Santa Isabella after the Spanish queen. A century later the Spaniards were driven out by the pirate José de Caspar, and Captiva was so called because his prisoners were kept there. The pirates were flushed out when the United States acquired Florida, and with the cultivation of sugarcane, tomatoes, and peaches the island flourished until a hurricane innundated Sanibel with salt water and ended its innings as farming country. Captiva evidently survived the disaster, for the trail

The old-timers reminisce nostalgically about the Island Inn—once a simple affair of rough cottages clustered round a dilapidated central block, each with a tap, bucket, and bench where the shellers could clean their catch and a nest of tables on which to display it. Sanibel Island. Photograph by Patrick Hodgson.

across its causeway is suddenly lined with burgeoning shrubs and overhung with magnificent trees and falls of vine, while the air is heavy with the scent of blossom. Close to the track some eaglets squeak from their nest in a sturdy tree. The parent bird soaring overhead has a white head, neck, and tail and yellow legs, which causes Terry and G to turn pink with pleasure, for this is a bald eagle, the American national emblem, a rare bird indeed and one in danger of extinction.

Soon we are picnicking on Captiva point, alone with one another, with the sea, sun, shore, shells, birds, and with one lady, as usual, bent double. Once before, when I was here with Pat, I asked him if he knew a certain woman by sight.

"I cannot be sure," he replied after a careful reconnaissance, "until I see her rump."

To walk over this beach is to feel for Jules Verne who wrote: "It is a great grief to crush under my foot the brilliant specimens of mollusk which strew the ground by thousands." This particular stretch is rich in classical pectens, the two halves of which are often in different colors. Sometimes one half is curved and the other flat. The flat half is known as the fan. Coquinas, like porcelain butterflies, ride in upon the waves and dig into the sand in a flash. If you are quick enough to catch them, they make an excellent broth. I find a shark's eye, a moonlike snail whose innocent appearance is belied by a powerful barbed tongue with which it punctures and devours clams and limpets. Thorny oysters abound, their valves held together by steely teeth. Unlike the pecten, their related shell which swims after its prey, these idlers moor themselves to a rock and catch their dinner as it passes.

The local names of many of the Florida shells are self-descriptive. The buttercup, for instance, with its canary yellow lining; the rose petal, nutmeg, Chinese alphabet, turkey wing, apple murex, tulip, rose cockle, lady's ear, elegant disk, bubble, checkerboard, cat's paw, jingle, boat shell, angel's wing, and so forth. This last shell, suitably named indeed when caught and cleaned by hands other than your own, dwells perversely some three feet deep in mud, the slimier the better. G declares that she was an ardent sheller until she and an angel's wing came to grips one evening on a mud bank. G won the first

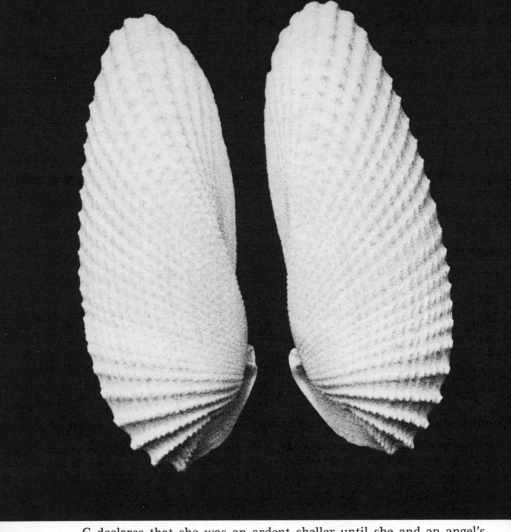

G declares that she was an ardent sheller until she and an angel's wing came to grips one evening on a mud bank. Photograph by Sara Heaton.

round. She caught him and got him home to the bathroom. Here, a very unangelic experience indeed awaited her. Even her steely determination wavered before its internal conglomeration of eye, testicle, stomach, blancmange, and a three-foot tube.

At Siesta Key the beach is remarkable for the quality of its milk-white sand, which, remarks Terry as we loll upon it at ease, is so exceptionally fine that a specimen of it was sent to Harvard to be analyzed. The finding was that it is 99 percent pure quartz grain. Quartz is graded as seven in the hardness scale of ten, the diamond being graded as ten. The minuscule size of the grain produces a floury texture that is particularly painless to stroll upon barefoot. G was doing precisely this one morning when she trod upon a buried stingray. It lashed at her with its formidable tail, which terminates in a poisoned barb. Pouring with blood and with her leg swelling to alarming proportions, she was borne off in agonizing pain and in some danger to the intensive care unit of the nearest hospital, where she was given a suitable antidote and the wound was successfully cauterized.

The inevitable shell shop at Siesta Key is run by a craggy old lady who looks not unlike a mollusk herself. She has raked through every creek and cove from Sarasota down to the south-ernmost key. Entombed within a glass case gleam the glories of Florida—the junonia and the lion's paw. I have already described the former, a cream-colored volute adorned with purplish brown spots, with a sensitively curved aperture; the latter is a magnificent pecten in tawny oranges and browns, its eight claws radiating outward in classical symmetry. Two junonias we have—Pat recently found a prize specimen on a mud bank off Marco—but we have no lion's paw, and this one I am unable to resist.

Later I present it to him casually: "Look what I found on the beach at Sarasota."

"Very nice. I suppose it stuck on its own price label?"

I also buy some shells too microscopic to gather on the shore and a herd of sea horses for my pictures. As a present for Terry I get a ghastly rosebud made from a single inverted shell, enameled orange with nail polish and mounted on a plastic stalk. He instantly appreciates its full horror and places it strategically in the drawing room, where it is inordinately admired by his luncheon guests.

"How clever you are, Terry, to grow a rose of such an un-usual color." (Terry is a dedicated gardener.)

"What a perfect rose, G." (Sniff.) "Mine have all got a blight this year."

147

At Siesta Key the beach is remarkable for the quality of its milk white sand, which is so exceptionally fine that a specimen of it was sent to Harvard to be analyzed. Photograph by Joseph Steinmetz shows sea oats in foreground.

The lion's paw (*Lyropectin nodosus*) is a magnificent pecten in tawny oranges and browns, its eight claws radiating outward in classical symmetry. Photograph by Sara Heaton.

To everyone's surprise but mine there is a violent storm in the night. (How Americans have the temerity to be so patronizing about the British climate never ceases to amaze me.)

"When's the season here?" I ask G.

She looks surprised. "The season's right now. January, February, March. Why?"

I put on an oilskin and one of those plastic head covers that make you look like something out of the fridge, grasp the relevant equipment, and stagger down to the beach. A seering wind is blowing inshore and violent waves are pounding on the rocks while mountains of spume rise like a bubble bath from every pool. Various crafty citizens, for whom such weather offers an unrepeatable opportunity, are creeping bent double along the ocean verge, poking in pools, overturning rocks, and chasing rolling shells into the backwash. Sometimes after a head-on encounter there is some reserved communication.

"Say, what's them you've got?"

"A tulip—it's damaged. A dead bonnet and these beaten-up conches."

"I've gotta fig and this sunrise tellin, see, but there's a drill hole in it." No beachcomber will ever admit to a lucky find.

At the base of the sea wall I station myself upon a spit of rock where, in due course, I get a live ponderous ark covered in a black velvet fuzz, its comblike hinge teeth giving no quarter; a lightning whelk, the shell already referred to, which possesses a left-handed aperture, and a Florida fighting conch, an aggressive character with a clawlike operculum. I also get soaked to the skin.

"Any good here?" One of the crafty ones.

"No luck, and it's wet work."

This character turns out to be a colleague, a fabricator of shell pictures.

"I don't care if they're broken; see, I just paint 'em green and use 'em for leaves. These dead ones I use for petals. I cover 'em with my bride's nail polish and she gets real mad."

Last night's tempest is succeeded by another, after which I rise early enough to be first on the scene. The tide is low, revealing smooth black rocks, easy to negotiate and interspersed with fruitful pools that eventually yield a double lemon yellow jewel box that later requires a hammer and chisel to prise it open; lovely candy-striped coquinas like tiny butter-flies; and a lady's ear—an elegant coiled disk, the kind of ear that goes with a rose-petal skin and teeth like pearls.

The late Harry Dupont, whose comprehensive collection of west Florida shells adorns the Johann Fust library on nearby Boca Grande, also used to go beachcombing before breakfast. One morning he was confronted by two simultaneous situations. The first was a glimpse of a school of live lion's paws marooned high on the shore by the falling tide. The second was a menace to them from the opposite direction by two elderly female collectors, bent double and loaded with businesslike equipment. His rivals had not yet spotted the prize but were nearer to it than Mr. Dupont and advancing at high speed. All is fair, or fairly fair, in such an emergency. The resourceful Mr. Dupont met it by becoming a pioneer streaker. He whipped off the belt supporting his bathing shorts, which sank to ankle level with a sigh of subsiding terylene acetate. Shielding their eyes, scandal-ized beyond utterance, the pair turned and mutely fled.

The houses at Siesta Key are ingeniously sited in fine gardens overlooking the ocean, the lagoon, or both, while a cosy club-house provides both a rendezvous and a retreat. Nevertheless, a positive explosion of creative talent has taken place here, which endows the atmosphere with a stimulating air of cut and thrust. Hardly a house is without its workshop, studio, music room or greenhouse, from which erupt carvings, sculp-ture, paintings, rare orchids, fine needlework, showers of musical notes, sheaves of manuscript, and connoisseurship in every form. And, of course, everyone gardens. In this soil all you need to do is to stick in a seed and then, like God, sit back and watch it grow—although, I am bound to admit, the seed is not the only thing that grows. "A garden is a lovesome thing,/ God wot!"/a lot of weeds.

Charles and Henrietta Winton's house, for instance, is an illustration of my theme, where I greatly admire some French Impressionists that turn out to have been painted by our

Shells from West Florida. Left to right, back row, Florida horse conch, Pacific thorny oyster; second row back, junonia; third row from back, two forms of sand dollars, lightning conch, double pecten, banded tulip, fighting conch; second row from front, junonia; front row, lion's paw, Atlantic coquinas, sea horses, murex. Photograph by Joseph Steinmetz.

hostess. Some chaste Chinese Immortals made of shells are also by her. A model of their yacht over the chimney piece has been carved and rigged by Charles, and by him also are some flotsam arrangements of driftwood. Meanwhile, some aptly named guests, Buck and Comfort O'Connor, gradually reveal their expertise on a variety of subjects, including Provençal

cooking. (We are subsequently to sample Comfort's bouilla-
baisse. A moving experience.) Among all these terrestial
preoccupations, the eyes of my vis-à-vis at table, Rufus Rand,
seem to be fixed upon affairs celestial. After gaining his earthly
wings in the first war, he became one of seven who supported
Charles Lindbergh's solo flight of the Atlantic. Lindbergh,
it appears, came from a hamlet near Minnesota called Little
Falls, the son of an embittered radical farmer of Swedish
birth. He earned his living by barnstorming the countryside,
demonstrating stunt-flying, wing-walking and parachuting. Later
he flew short, mean, bad-weather flights for the post office,
all the time preaching the potentiality of long-distance aviation
into ears that would not hear. When at last Doctor Lister, of
mouthwash fame, Rufus Rand, and others were sufficiently
convinced, they subscribed among them for the famous plane
The Spirit of St. Louis.

Breathes there a man with a soul so dead who never to
himself hath said, one of these days I should like to see that
fabulous iron lacework on the Creole homesteads in New
Orleans? The map reveals that it is perfectly possible to head
for home via Louisiana and Mississippi taking in, magical words,
the *vieux carré.* From New Orleans it is not difficult, although
circuitous, to board a plane and stay with it until it finds London
some fourteen hours later. Well, why not? Travel is said to
broaden the beam.

"Da Vinci's Last Supper—8 miles," proclaims a billboard on
route for the airport. I had no idea we were so near Milan.

Early in the eighteenth century a certain Jean Baptiste Le
Moyne become governor of the French colony of Lousiana,
so called for le Roi Soleil. His aim, to establish a trading center
there, was eventually accomplished in the cypress swamp of
Biloxi, presently called Orleans after the duke of that name,
but it failed to prosper. So tedious and unhealthy had the
poor man's existence become that he engaged a M. de la Tour
to plan a city on the coast along French lines, or rather French

croissants, and the Crescent City of New Orleans was established. In 1762 the Spanish moved in, but by 1800 had retroceded Louisiana to France, and, in 1803, Napoleon, who needed fifteen million dollars for the invasion of England, sold Louisiana to President Jefferson for that sum. This was the famous Louisiana Purchase. The nefarious British next made a bid to control the Mississippi valley but were ignominiously defeated in 1814 by Andrew Jackson's Kentucky Riflemen. In 1861, the growing threat from the north to abolish slavery caused the states carved from Lousiana Purchase to join with Florida and declare their independence, adopting as their symbol the ill-fated banner of the Confederacy. The southern way of life, which meant the economy of these states, was based on slave labor in the cotton fields, to defend which the plantation owners unhesitatingly engaged in civil war against the detested Yankees who threatened it. Well, the slaves eventually threw off their chains, a sigh of relief ran round those civilized countries whose economics were not so based, and the cotton plantations and all they stood for sank slowly into the rubescent mud.

"Think Green!" advises a huge billboard dominating the highway into New Orleans. I obey and narrowly avert an attack of jaundice.

"We get sixty-three inches of rain every goddam year," announces my cabdriver, gazing cheerfully between the threshing windshield wipers. "New Orleans is built right on a swamp, but it ain't sunk yet. That's why we don't get no hippies here!" He grins delightedly. "I guess they jest don't like water. Last week we had sixteen inches in seventeen hours." He mounts the pavement momentarily, in a long skid. "Sidewalks here, ma'am, are called banquettes."

The population is a mixture of French, Irish, Spanish, German, and Italian. What they call here the "true" Creole is a person descended from settlers born in Louisiana before the Purchase.

We now enter the *vieux carré*, a somewhat self-conscious district of eighteenth-century houses illuminated by torchlight and embellished with fanlights, graceful fenestration, and balconies of filigree ironwork. Horse-drawn surreys with fringed awnings add an air of improbability to the scene. At the hub of the quarter stands the Royal Orleans Hotel, a classical structure of considerable dignity, a sanctum of comfort. Southern belles by the dozen with their escorts, Creoles to the fingertips, languish in its colonnaded halls sipping iced mint juleps from frosted beakers. Gone with the wind, borne back on the breeze. Indeed, the next day we are shown the very mansion in which Scarlett O'Hara and Rhett Butler were united in matrimony, if united is the word.

The old town was burned down in 1788, so most of the architecture dates from after that year. The classical facades of the mansions standing in courtyards glowing with camellia and magnolia conceal, however, sordid slave quarters at the rear. In the ruins of one splendid mansion in Royal Street, the fire revealed spiked collars, whips, and branding irons that were used by the lady of the house herself on slaves chained to the wall. The slave market still stands and in those days was open daily for exchange or sale.

After Napoleon lost the battle of Waterloo, the French community decided to offer him the crown of Louisiana and set about preparing a palace worthy of him, but he died at St. Helena before the proposition was made. His physician, Antommarch, cast the emperor's death mask and sent this instead to the governor of New Orleans.

The cathedral, much restored, is late railway station Gothic. Over the altar a vast smoke-blackened picture dimly discloses St. Francis in the throes of receiving what the guide describes as the "astigmata."

"Then I reckon Doctor Schneburgher can cure Emilia's eczema," is the curious comment made on this event by some oracle in the crowd.

The best thing in the whole town is an iron paling enclosing the garden of a clapboard house flanked with Ionic columns. It consists of a design of budding corn stalks entwined with morning glory that will at any moment surely burst into flower.

After the Purchase in 1802, the importance of the French

quarter began to diminish. The Americans proceeded to build their own quarter, now known as the garden district. The result is a tightly packed area of neoclassic mansions set among suffocating groves of trees and shrubs. An Irish guide called Mick bashes his sightseeing bus along the boulevards to the accompaniment of a commentary to catch the authentic flavor of which calls for a Hiberian ear.

"The rollcall of churches on this Avenoo is quite somethin'. Don't get sore, folks, if your fancy ain't come up yet. We got 'em somewhere. That one there like a slipped disk—that's the Baptist church. Over here's the funeral parlor. Those folks sure carry out everything they undertake. Here's the cemetery of St. Roche, patron of good health, ha, ha, and them dead as doornails. To dig a grave round here is to dig a well, so they all gotta get put above ground. That's why you're looking at a hundred and fifty acres of solid granite, folks, and boy, do I wish I had the contract!"

These observations are interspersed with damyankee stories at least a hundred years out of date. Perhaps they have not yet heard in New Orleans that the Civil War is over.

"Tonight's St. Patrick's Day, folks, the biggest day after Mardi Gras in this little 'ole town. Even the beer is dyed green." (He is not joking.) "I'll be glad to escort all you ladies to our night-life party. Tickets, ten dollars a knob. Striptease, the dance of elimination and temptation. The My Oh My Club. That's where all the girls are really boys, and that's what you'll say when you come out. My oh my."

The final stop is made before the gates of an ancient convent surrounded by a peaceful garden within crumbling stone walls. A woodpecker is tapping a fastidious route up the trunk of an oak tree. Under a magnolia laden with blossoms the size of soup plates waits a commodious iron chair. Disenchanted with Mick or Mike, whatever his name is, I defect from the tour to sit in the evening sun until it is extinguished by an indigo wall of rising cloud. A bell tolling from a nearby tower announces that the day is over and the hour is approaching for "dinner at Antoine's."

157

8 Mauritius

In the purple shadow cast by the Mountain of Morne, Mauritius, lies the Morne Brabant, the sort of hostelry now accepted as de luxe by the migratory hordes. It now shelters Pat, foundering in a deathlike trance after a twenty-four hour flight from the sceptered isle. I have just been roused from mine by a bird in the bathroom, a lizard on the ceiling, and a mosquito inside my net. I feebly seal up a hole in it with adhesive tape.

French windows open onto a straight mile of pallid beach and dark water, fringed with a foaming reef. I totter towards the ocean brink, across a stretch of white dust that gradually shades off into coarse amber sand. The beach is strewn with fat starfish, flesh-colored with livid spots, and gaily hued mussels clinging to one another in long odoriferous swags. It is not to consume *moules marinières* that we have flown half across the world, and with increasing exasperation I search for nonexistent traces of other species. The splendid collection sent to me by my unknown correspondent in John o'Groats came from this island and, unless conditions have changed since the days of her deceased great-aunt, similar specimens must surely abound somewhere.

An angular Indo-Frenchman with ice grey eyes, Jean-Claude by name, materializes across my path. He is wearing a pith helmet that would cause Mr. Lock of St. James's to revolve in his grave like a roulette wheel.

"Does Madame seek a boat?"

Madame has sought many a boat without so much as a whiff of a shell at the end of it, so she conducts the conversation with caution. With Gallic fervor, Jean-Claude describes distant mud flats positively crawling with shells. Particularly harps, he insists; sometimes, indeed, imperial harps. Also they crawl, it seems, on the lee of yonder point and to the east of that far island. Tomorrow morning shall we not need him, Madame, with his glass-bottom boat and his diving equipment? Done, Jean-Claude! And done is the word.

At morning light Jean-Claude, having forgotten his diving gear, chuffs up in a rowboat with a outboard motor and, having conveyed us about three hundred yards, prepares to dump us upon the hotel reef.

"Is this where you are taking us?"

"Today it is best here," he declares with a shrug, "and Madame had better take off her trousers," he adds, scanning my Abercrombie and Fitch denims. Having on only pink drawers underneath, I disregard this advice and step overboard with a crunch of collapsing coral. Jean-Claude indifferently wades off to fish for his own dinner. Here abound many an old chum—the spotted snake, the black sea slug, the bloated pink ditto with bristles, and hosts of sea urchins with quills like knitting needles. I am gratified, however, to corner a modest Hebrew cone and a juvenile heart cockle. The tide is rumored to be going out but is clearly coming in. As the water deepens, gusts of wind and rain begin to chase one another across the ocean face. Opening my memsahib's parasol from Harrods (tussore, with bottle-green lining), which I find invaluable as a rod and staff and for poking in holes, my bosom is invaded by darkish doubts. Some joker in London declared that the temperature in Mauritius hardly varies the year round but, say what he will, August is winter here and it is exceedingly cool. Only the ubiquitous mosquito endures. (Resolve: After this I am through with reefs, and this time I mean it.) I wave the parasol to communicate my intention of regaining the boat and having a question asked in the House of Commons about the climate, when Jean-Claude is suddenly seen to be involved in mortal combat with a threshing moray eel. Pat and I can only gape in frozen horror.

"Keep away! He's dangerous!" bawls Jean-Claude, somewhat unnecessarily, struggling with a zeal matched only by that of the moray eel to dislodge it from the end of the stick upon which it is impaled. Disengaged at last, we catch the flash of two stone-cold serpent eyes before it whips out of sight, trailing behind it a long plume of blood.

As we chug towards the shore, Jean-Claude notices our all but empty bags and, with relish, produces from under the seat a crate of gleaming shells for which he demands an astronomical sum. We glare at him and at them, determined to find our own or bust. He is blithely unaware when he disposes us waterlogged on the beach that this is goodbye to him, his boat, and his dinner (a dead octopus). No barge pole exists long enough for us not to touch them with.

After dinner, under an oddly tilted moon, we join a shivering group of spectators of some exponents of the national dance, the *sega*. So unlovely a performance can only be authentic. The troupe consists of four African couples clad in faded cotton, the men with battered hats crammed low upon their brows. With foreheads almost touching, they watch their own feet shuffling and stamping to the furious rhythm of a native drum. It looks dead monotonous and dead easy, but turns out to be neither. The master of ceremonies in tattered red breeches, with the low profile of Napoleon in exile, beckons us to the floor.

"Like so!" he cries, feet spurting like fireworks, hips weaving, a lank lock of hair springing on his forehead. It's all very well to say like so. Handicapped by a skin-tight evening dress, high-heeled sandals, and a failure to catch the rhythm, I am overcome with terpsichorean prissiness. It's no good. Nothing will waggle. Napoleon, uttering short barks, is undulating opposite me like a cobra about to strike, but he soon deserts me for a more rewarding partner, apparently without a spinal column.

In so polyglot an atmosphere it is difficult to discover which race is indigenous here, and research discloses that none are. References to the island by early Phoenicians and Arabs record that they found it unpopulated. The first European to establish himself here was a Portuguese captain in the fifteenth century, who christened it the Island of the Swan after his ship. A

The Dutch made history by extinguishing the dodo, a fowl of an unusually trusting nature. British Museum of Natural History. London.

few years later it was taken over by the Dutch who renamed it Mauritius, after Prince Maurice of Nassau, and proceeded to stock up their ships with deer and game in such quantities that they made history by extinguishing the dodo, a fowl of an unusually trusting nature. In 1710 the Dutch were suceeeded by the French who, from the shelter of Port Louis, were prone to harry British traders en route to India, until the British seized it from Napoleon in 1810. For strategic and trade reasons the British stuck to Mauritius after Napoleon's fall but followed a policy that was intended to be a generous one. Gallic civilization and tradition were to be respected, and the sugar-cane plantations were to remain in French hands.

THE SPELL OF THE SHELL

The actual government of the island, however, was to be carried out from Whitehall through a resident governor. In effect, the island gradually fell between two stools. The economy was based on forced labor in the sugar industry, and the French planters clung to slavery long after it had been abolished elsewhere. When the British finally forced abolition on them, the planters who did not go bankrupt imported cheap Indian labor instead. Criminals and dropouts from the slums of Bombay, existing on a pittance in indescribable squalor, were soon in the majority on the island. Between these Indians who now dominated the sugar industry and the liberated Africans, a violent antagonism developed. The Indians themselves were divided by fanatical internecine strife between Hindu and Moslem. The French aristocratic families either sold out or withdrew to France and became absentee landlords. The remaining French and the British detested each other and declined even to dine in one another's company.

When we drive inland towards the central plateau to escape the cold wind, we find a huge checkerboard of cane fields aswarm with Indians. They are immersed in the unending cycle of clearing the earth, setting the seedlings, and hacking down the ripe cane with machetes. Entombed within the stillness of the stony fields, the laborers keep their eyes passively downward upon their interminable task. No hand is raised in greeting, seldom do you see a smile, never a laugh. On the long bare roads, legions of soft-footed Indian women, erect as caryatids, their saris flowing behind them, bear on their heads bundles of firewood or sheaves of rushes for the goats or for the sacred cow. How hauntingly unhappy seems this so-called island in the sun! Even in the fashionable suburbs, gangs of young unisexuals, with straight flowing hair and gaudy sweaters loaf on street corners staring after the passersby with boredom and frustration stamped on every feature.

The city of Curepipe, the objective of this expedition, sprang up almost overnight to accommodate refugees from a epidemic of malaria which, in the 1860s, ran through the island like the Black Death. The mountain climate offered almost complete immunity from the fever, and the mushroom town and its suburbs matured into the principal residential areas. Although the purlieus contain some fine houses set in flourishing gardens, the city itself suffers from a total lack of charm. A pseudo-Gothic cathedral robustly spears the clouds with a stout steeple; jerry-building, neon lighting, garish billboards, and canned music assail the senses; underbred dogs rootle among the garbage, and mute beggars crouch in doorways with extended hands. Investigation, however, reveals a courtly and fair-dealing Chinese shopkeeping community, no strangers to taste and to the fine arts, owning backstreet shops bulging with porcelain, coromandel, gems, tapestry, and jade. I acquire from one an ivory pagoda hung with tiny bells, destined to throw a Brighton Pavilion shadow across the dark coral wall of my bedroom at home, to keep company with a yellow Chinese Immortal.

The return journey leads us past a couple of tempting beaches, one of which is dominated by a noticeboard that observes with laconic simplicity: "If you bathe here you will be drowned." At the other we fill one of my shoes with microscopic shells like beads of lapis lazuli and emerald. On the approach to the Morne Brabant, Pat nearly throws me through the windscreen, having suddenly espied a pyramid of shells on a roadside stall. Among them reposes the glory of the Mauritian shores—a violet spider conch.

In Bhojoo, or Bobby, we have found our rainbow's end. Morne Brabant, Mauritius. Photograph by Patrick Hodgson.

163

"How much?" The shell's purple flush has faded and it lacks luster, but it is nevertheless the genuine article.

"It's no good. It was dead when I found it."

For the first time Pat meets the lively eyes and engaging grin of Mr. Bhojoo Maneeram. We do not yet know it but in Bhojoo, or Bobby, we have found our rainbow's end. Since he graduated from his mother's knee he has earned his daily bread, by finding and cleaning shells, and the reefs are as familiar to him as his own backyard. Meanwhile the conversation follows a familiar pattern. Yes, he owns a boat with an outboard motor and will bring his diving gear. Yes, there are shells on the lee of that point, on the east of the Ile aux Benètiers, and on those mudflats, but you must get up early.

"What do you call early?"

"You must be on the reef at six."

"We shall probably get here about eight."

"No, no! Seven then."

So it evolves that next morning we find ourselves plodding across a mudflat towards a rough-hewn boat, prinked up with a flossy outboard, anchored off the hamlet of La Gaulette. Soon we are blinding across the bay towards an invisible reef, upon which we presently run gently aground. The men swing themselves overboard and stand knee-deep in the fast running water.

"D'you want a hand?"

"I'm not coming."

"Not coming? What are you going to do?"

"Sit here and write my book."

They both goggle at me, obviously seeking symptoms of derangement; then, shaking their heads in bewilderment, they resignedly squelch away. Presently they are to be seen bent double, stumbling into pools and reaching shoulder-deep into crevices, two apposite dots upon the horizon.

I ferret out a massive shell, sensibly named a bailer, and dispose of about nine inches of water sloshing about in the bottom of the boat. Then seated on the floor boards, my sun-shade lifted against passing squalls, and with pen poised over pad, I make a careful appraisal of the ambience. Colette's advice to the aspiring writer is as follows:

I sat in the boat and wrote my book. The reef Mauritius. Photograph by Patrick Hodgson.

Only describe what you have seen. Look long and hard at the things that please you, even longer and harder at the things that give you pain. Be faithful to your first impression. . . . Do not wear yourself out by telling lies.

Even the truth is wearing enough. Apple green water reels across the reef between menacing outcrops of coral. Occasionally a deadly kiss from one of these dances through the hull as the boat swings on its anchor. The surface of the sea looks like a kettle about to boil over.

A blood red starfish, a bonnet de prêtre, sweeps past among a stream of transparent shrimps. A bumpily shaped fish wavers by, orange and lemon. Tufts of teased-out cotton-wool clouds

plume aimlessly across the sky in discreditable disorder. I
look long and hard, as recommended, and am well satisfied
with my billet at the bottom of the boat. Eventually Pat and
Bobby, soaked to the armpits, approach within earshot. "There's
a cowry by your left foot, Monsieur."

"Where? I can't see it."

"Just where you are looking."

"What, that? Surely that's a stone?"

Bobby pounces on a humpback cowry before it has time to
withdraw its foot and pavonian mantle between its formidable
teeth. But, once folded away within its porcelain fastness, the
cowry gleams in Bobby's grasp in full perfection. Altogether,
I rather fancy the lifestyle of the cowry. No housing problem
clouds its horizon, nor is it concerned with income tax,
delinquency or appointments with the dentist. The human being,
on the other hand, encased within its envelope of tender and
vulnerable flesh, is endlessly subject to passion, to fashion,
and to worse.

The tide is now slipping off the shoulder of some basalt
rocks through which Bobby cautiously nudges a path, to lollop
across the channel to the Ile aux Benètièrs. The scene is the usual
one of marine desolation. The beaches are strewn with lobster
legs, crab shells, disintegrating scrub, and bleaching bones—not,
I trust, those of the saintly hermit said to live in a cave on
the southern shore. From amongst the rubble we idly garner
a couple of whelklike shells. We are electrified to see that their
whorls descend in a sinestral manner. Except for the lightning
whelk, a shell common to the west coast of Florida, all
properly conducted shells operate in a clockwise direction.
Thus our thoughts stray towards the London sales where
freaks command a stiff price. Pat also comes upon an onion
tun, a highly descriptive term for the white bulbous shell
etched with light brown ribs. But his best find is a flattened
brown, black, and white spiral, called the perspective sundial.
It is in mint condition and measures at least three inches
across, the largest specimen Bobby has ever seen. It will break,
alas, in the process of being boiled to extract the creature.
Suddenly Bobby's attention is attracted by a hole in the sand
winking with water. He flings himself upon it, digging frantically

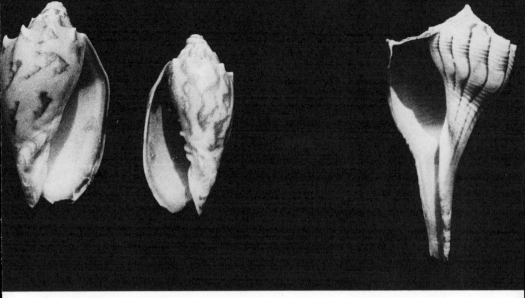

Except for the lightning whelk (right), a shell common to the west coast of Florida, all properly conducted shells operate in a clockwise direction. Photograph by Sara Heaton.

like a terrier after a rat. Triumphantly he hauls out today's dinner, a *crabe c'est ma faute,* a lopsided customer with one enormous yellow and red claw, the other in embryo, like a bud.

Speaking of dinners, binges for our feathered friends are becoming a daily solace as one inclement morning succeeds another. Starting at breakfast with toast and cornflakes, by lunchtime they have graduated to a menu of half of a coconut followed by bacon, sausage, and raspberry jam. Sparrows, canaries, and some little dappled fellows with tip-tilted black crests all too quickly gain confidence and are soon flying in and out of our bedroom at ease, as if it were a club, leaving behind copious mementos of their membership. An outer ring of ill-disposed crows observe the goings-on with harshly expressed disapproval. Every now and then, greatly daring, one will dart in among the busily pecking birds, seize some outsize titbit and stagger with it out of range, where, squawking furiously it will drive off all comers with villainous pecks.

167

These Franciscan preoccupations are observed from afar by a distraught-looking old gentleman, a Mr. Malcolm Chaqadzl, a painter of some note, we are told, but a recluse. One evening, investigating the source of a contralto voice singing somewhere in the moonlight, we come upon him seated in the woods having dinner served to him on a card table. He is nattily dressed in a city suit, button boots, a woollen muffler, and a trilby hat with a feather in it.

"I always eat here alone," he remarks chattily as soon as we are within earshot. "I hate people who talk. Quack, quack, quack. I like only to paint. Have you seen my paintings?"

We regret infinitely that we have not. He has an exhibition somewhere and urges an early visit upon us.

"My paintings are the paintings of innocence. Ninety percent of children who see them understand them, 60 percent of women, men almost never—don't ask me why." He glares at Pat, who refrains from so asking. "A tree is a person, a house is a person," he continues, filling his lungs as if he were about to take high D. "So is a telephone, a table, a chair, a pair of boots. A flower has a face and eyes. (Curried lobster please, Sharif, and some black coffee.) A tree has arms and legs. A mountain breathes, a stone moves."

There seems no valid comment to be made on these observations, but we are spared the necessity of finding some riposte by the owner of the contralto voice, now singing in Persian, advancing through the trees in full song. With hand on hip, the singer pauses before us. Presently there is a climax to be attained, and she attains it before ending on a long drawn-out throbbing note.

"Bravo!, Bravo!"

"I love to be alone in the woods," she remarks beaming delightedly. "People who talk get on my nerfs. Cackle, cackle, cackle. I like only to sing. In Iran I sing much in the opera and also in the concert."

There seems little else to be done after this but repair to our ruin on the fruit machines, leaving the pair of them together chattering like monkeys.

"Pat, quick!" (Bash on the bathroom door). "A four-pointed starfish has just been washed upon the beach!"

168

"Well, what am I expected to do about it?"

"Come and pick him up."

"I'm shaving for God's sake! You pick him up."

"I can't. He gives me the pink horrors."

"Stop being so squeamish."

Silence, save for the sound of waters finding their own level. *Après lui le deluge.* Back on location, I gather and interlace together three sticks, scoop up the starfish, and bear him homeward, a perfect nine-inch cross of pink sausage. Graham, the six-year-old son of a Capetown biologist, crosses the triumphal route.

"I too," he confides coolly, after subjecting my prize to a brief professional scrutiny, "am interested in echinodermata."

An increasing portion of each day is spent in the company of the Maneeram family. It consists of parents who live "behind the house"; of their fisherman son, Jack; his wife, Leila, who cannot read or write and can barely speak; and their two babies, Sabine and Bobo. Then comes Bobby, followed by a younger brother, Jim. Their modern bungalow backs onto the sea from which the family draw their sustenance—fish, lobsters, and crabs for the market, and shells which they sell from strategically placed roadside stalls. They operate as a closely integrated team with Bobby as undisputed leader. The older brothers are on the reef every morning at dawn, as by now we know all too well. The youngest, Jim, rears rabbits, hens, and goats and runs the shell stalls, for which Bobby pays him more than a cane cutter gets for a ten-hour day. The old father grows the fruit and vegetables, the downtrodden Leila cleans the shells, minds her babies, and does the household chores, while her mother-in-law tends the holy cow. Bobby, whose income is double that of the accountant in the hotel, carries out some mysterious transaction in Port Louis, the capital, once a week. On Sunday night he patronizes a fishcotheque in Curepipe where, no doubt, he rocks and rolls to the strains of the Water Music. Although the prospect of being tied to one woman for life appalls him, he admits to a girl friend. His gimlet eye never misses a pretty face or an arched foot with a ring on its toe. Allah he ignores altogether, except for a passing prayer on a matter of business.

Rounding up the fish traps before the market opens. Mauritius.
Photograph by Patrick Hodgson.

At the outset, our expeditions to the reefs with Bobby
began at a tolerable hour after bath and breakfast, but his iron
will has gradually prevailed.

It is not long before we are being awakened before daybreak and are to be observed wading through icy water towards
Jack's boat, fretting at its mooring, to round up the fish traps
before the market opens. This routine involves four or five
hours of sitting on a plank among fish and mollusks in their
last throes, creeping crustacea, fish bait, traps, tackle, and wet
shoes. It is a delightful arrangement for the Maneeram Co.,
Ltd., for we pay them by the hour for a boat that they are
using for their own purposes as well. But the new dimension

of reef life that Bobby has opened up for us is beyond price, and one in which physical discomfort is immaterial. This dread hour before the sun rises is when the creatures come out to feed, and for the first time we see them living and moving, wonderfully and fearfully made, master builders whose architectural miracles embody the basis of a multitude of mathematically correct vaults, arches, staircases, porticos, and niches. Peering through the water, he shows us how to follow the feathery trail of the miter shell to its focal point; how to pierce the camouflage of, to us, invisible cowries and helmets; how to track down the collector's item, the imperial harp. Astonishingly, this is a huge pink jellyfish, its shell, containing all its vitals, perched at its center like a howdah on an elephant. Bobby knows exactly where the feeding grounds of the olives

The astonishing Venus' comb (*Murex pecten*), a shell covered with a hundred needle-sharp spines, so artfully placed that any sensible predator would think twice before attempting a first bite. Photograph by Sara Heaton.

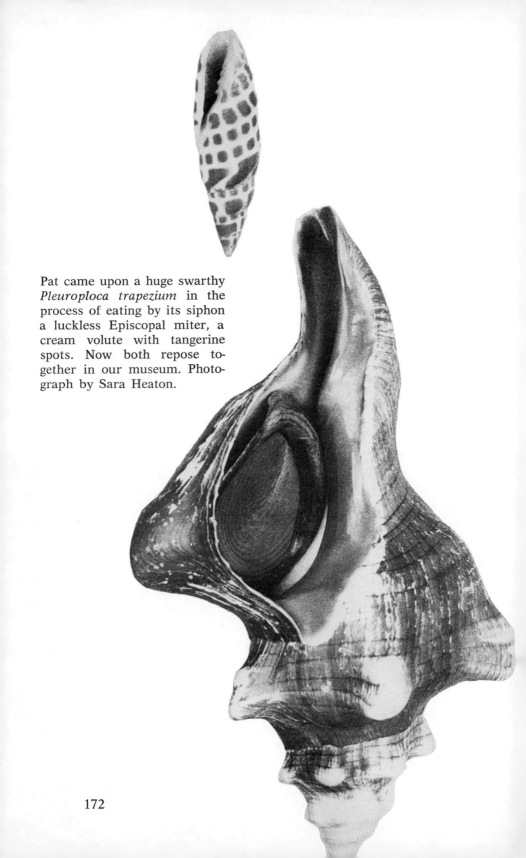

Pat came upon a huge swarthy
Pleuroploca trapezium in the
process of eating by its siphon
a luckless Episcopal miter, a
cream volute with tangerine
spots. Now both repose together in our museum. Photograph by Sara Heaton.

172

are, where we can see them undulating across the sand, the design on their shells exactly corresponding with those on their mantles. Here, he also digs up the astonishing Venus' comb, a shell covered with a hundred needle-sharp spines, so artfully placed that any sensible predator would think twice before attempting a first bite, for it would surely be its last. Fascinated we see how the sea anemone gathers its victim into its wavering embrace, and how the mollusks prey upon one another. Diving on to a sandy bottom about a fathom deep, Pat comes upon a huge swarthy *Pleuroploca trapezium*, with its blood-red entrails fully extended, in the process of eating by its siphon a luckless Episcopal miter, a cream volute with tangerine spots. Now both repose together in our museum, joined in the everlasting kiss of death. One time, while investigating under a rocky ledge where schools of bourse and of waggling *sacre chien rouge* were foraging, I am disconcerted to find myself gazing into a pair of beadlike eyes out on stalks, rising from a cluster of spines. A scientific description of this pincushion is beyond me. I feel like the child who, asked to describe an elephant, answered, "I cannot describe the elephant but I know one when I see it."

The sex life of the mollusk as described to us by Bobby seems singularly unrewarding. Oysters, for instance, change their sex annually—male one year, female the next, which must be very unsettling. (This revelation caused me to examine closely the next dozen Whitstables I ate, dished out to me in English's Oyster Bar in Brighton by Fred, who won a cup for being the fastest oyster opener in Europe. These oysters were either all boys or all girls, for they looked and tasted identical.) Then a few species of mollusks are hermaphrodites, and fertilize themselves with their own sperm. Very dull. Certain embryos, enclosed protectively within their mother's shell, eat one another until the strongest emerges alone, a solitary but well-nourished individual. A few species retain their eggs within their shell until the brood is ready to hatch out, when they give birth to living and perfectly formed young. Some bivalves, those which live in mangrove swamps, will breed only during the first high tide after the full moon—while yet other mollusks will lay only when the temperature rises above 60° F. But the great majority simply release their sperm or eggs, according to their current sex, into the uncaring waters where, in a catch as catch can fashion, they unite or perish.

For the last week Mauritius has lain in the pall of a cyclone said to be raging over Madagascar, but today the sky is arched with rainbows, and for the first time fleets of towering clouds begin to sail away into the blue. The air develops a sharp, almost an Alpine quality; it becomes a day on which to think in terms of mountain tops which, a map discloses, can be reached by a series of long S-curves rising from sea level to peter out somewhere in mid-Mauritius. Our mustard colored mini buzzes confidently upward, attaining peak after peak of oddly shaped summits which, even at this altitude, are arrayed in steeply sloping fields of sugar cane.

Pat looks uneasy. "Are your ears singing?"

"Singing?" I listen intently. "Something is, but I don't think its me."

He switches off the engine and the silence is charged with a low-pitched vibration that gradually increases in volume as we begin to trace it to its source on foot. Eventually we are confounded by the sight of a vast waterfall, dropping five hundred feet sheer into a narrow gorge, with a roar like Hyde Park Corner. In a flash of enlightenment I know that when, under some other sky, I enact my unthinking role—being, observing, feeling, sleeping—I shall be aware from time to time of this torrent, endlessly pouring itself over the monumental cliff. I become conscious also of the extent of our isolation, half a mile off a track in central Mauritius, somewhere in Sinbad's forgotten sea of Zanj. It gives me quite a turn. Suppose one of us should pull a tendon or spring a leak?

Lifting up mine eyes unto the serrated hills, I muse upon the peculiar mold in which they are cast, going up where you confidently expect them to be coming down. And now I come to think of it, it is not only the mountains. The zebu are also the wrong shape. They are either buffalo with a waning hump or cattle with a waxing one. Then consider the dodo! Sometimes it weighed as much as fifty pounds, and it combined the body of

an ostrich with short legs and rudimentary wings. (Being innocent of fear and inquisitive by temperament, it came to investi- ,
gate the Dutch, and was quickly caught, eaten, and extinct.)
As for the bumpy bourse fish, you can hardly tell whether it
is coming or going, while Pat met a quite preposterous tortoise
when taking an evening stroll. It must have been at least five
feet long. Somehow the design here has got off key.

Two Indian ladies are sitting companionably under a banyan
tree, each extracting nits from the head of the other. A canary-
yellow bird with an ebony throat is expressing itself on a jarring
note upon some upper branch, from which fibrous rope pours
down, rooting itself in the soil and, springing upward again,
producing continuous banyan. This brings to mind a horticul-
tural friend of ours, John Codrington, for whom a seed from
this tree might be just the thing. Eventually we deliver one to
him in a matchbox.

"You didn't pick it off the tree I hope?"

"Of course we did, where else?"

"It won't grow unless it has been through a bird," is his
dusty answer.

As we cross an escarpment we see the silhouette of a monolithic deer, splendidly antlered, a sitting shot. Thousands of
these Cervus elaphus—they weight at least three hundred
pounds—roam the mountains where *la chasse* is a very chic
preoccupation, if *chasse* is the word. The huntsmen sit in
redoubts built in trees, furnished with books, booze, and
luncheon baskets, and take potshots at the deer when they are
flushed out by beaters and hounds. Incidentally, the venison
on the menu last night had not been hung long enough and
tasted like tough shoe. The cuisine, in fact, despite the French
tradition, is not the long suit of this island. Torture by slave
cookery has been succeeded by reliance upon Indians who
merely add curry to whatever ingredients are available, or upon
African cooks who do not even do that.

"Everything all right, sah?" enquires our African waiter radiantly, thinking nothing of interrupting some absorbing conversation. What is the answer to this? It is very far from all right.
It is revolting.

"Fine, thank you, Mahomed Ali." His name is the equivalent of being called Jesus God.

A dead straight highway runs forty miles south along the coast to the capital, Port Louis, which, cradled in the amphitheatre of the Moka mountains, endures a climate like a cauldron and drips with humidity. A former governor, Sir John Pope-Hennessey, had sensibly moved the residency to a comfortable Georgian house in the hills, from which eminence he and his successors were able to conduct their affairs in safety and in a bracing climate. The 1860 epidemic of malaria at sea level already described, had been immediately followed by the worst hurricane on record. Mercury sank from sight in barometers, whirlwinds alternated with blinding downpours of rain, the ocean developed a sinister swell, and all the birds winged madly out to sea. It struck on the Ides of March, raged for three days, and veered off again, leaving the island a total shambles.

All this is described to us in a dramatic manner by a chance acquaintance, a Mauritian businessman whom I shall call Benjamin. We sit together, under a towering Latania palm (which only flowers once, after which it immediately perishes) overlooking a lake covered with water lily leaves the size of flying saucers. Very immoderate, the equator. He explains in French that this island, in spite of independence, remains illogically attached to Britain, which seems to have caused it to go somewhat off beam. Too many M.P.'s are chasing too few citizens— and the postponement of the election has resulted in a virtual dictatorship. Dictatorship by whom? Benjamin, who is an M.P. himself, avoids this pitfall and murmurs uneasily that certain foreign elements are stirring up factions.

Factions? Well, yes. It seems by the end of the last century at least 200,000 people found themselves squeezed into Mauritius, which is about one-sixth the size of Jamaica. They consisted mostly of newly enfranchised African slaves who instantly became fishermen or small holders farming their own land, and of Indian laborers, recruited to replace them and exploited even farther than the slaves had been. Although both speak in French, the overtones are British. They range in color from cream to the blackest of black coffee. Mauritius in fact, is not truly home to the descendants of either of these races. Perhaps this is why they crouch in the doorways of their hovels staring out with tragic black eyes. Maybe they are visualizing some distant Eldorado, which they know only too well would repudiate them. Even the well-established Benjamin seems to share the general unrest, for as we drive towards Port Louis he sounds us out about the possibility of work in London. This is a familiar theme to Pat, who is already under pressure from other Mauritians in various walks of life, all of whom yearn to emigrate, preferably to England or the United States, but almost anywhere will do.

"But what on earth's that?" interrupts Pat, strategically changing the subject, as a confused mirage of towers crowds across our vision.

"It's a hospital." We gaze incredulously through the windshield. I know of nothing to compare with it in size outside of New York. "It cost many millions. We've hardly any doctors or nurses, so no patients. It's got all the latest equipment, which nobody on the island knows how to work or maintain. One of your specialists said that it's a hospital worthy of the center of London, a great teaching hospital—but already the white ants are eating it."

After a pause he adds with a shrug: "I'll show you how we Mauritians keep healthy."

Obediently, we clatter after him down a cobbled alley into the market, where among the vegetables he pauses before a stall which proclaims: "Messrs. Naiken, père et fils, avec un demi-siècle d'expèrience." A profusion of sweet-smelling fresh herbs, flowers and roots are on display, some ground into powder, others dried into tisanes, all of them destined to ease such burdens of mankind as *la colique, hépatique, pierres, gaz, foie, coeur,* tension, oppression, depression, *froid, energic,* and *diarrhée.*

Our life on the reefs with Bobby flows on daily in full perfection under a sky continually crisscrossed with rainbows, but social intercourse with him is not without pitfalls. Several times he has come with us to Port Louis when, glowingly handsome

177

Our life on the reefs with Bobby flows on daily. Mauritius.

with his finely cut features, glossy black hair, and graceful figure, he usually manages to look rather better dressed than Pat.

"I sit here and wait," he announces on one occasion, indicating a banquette in the hall of the restaurant in which we are about to have lunch. We look at him in dismay. It has already been arranged that he is to be our guest. Is he afraid of the scowling Indian proprietor, or is someone throwing an unclean shadow over something?

"Don't be ridiculous, Bobby. Sit down with us and decide what you want."

Meanwhile, in the short time available, I am trying to instill a thirst for scholarship into Leila, Bobby's sister-in-law. Having acquired some elementary books we sit daily on the back doorsteps grappling with the ABCs.

"Pea for Pig." Silence.

"Pea, Leila, say Pea."

"Pea," she obliges, giggling. Pig seems to be beyond her.

"Pea for Pig," echoes Sabine, aged three, hopping with nits, leaning radiantly against my knee.

Bobby hovers in the background. He does not approve of Leila being given ideas above her station.

A sky continually crisscrossed with rainbows. Mauritius. Photograph by Martha Hodgson.

"Beat her if she does not do what you say," he suggests revealingly.

Walking on the beach before breakfast one morning, I meet a French boy emerging from the sea with a bag suspended from his neck full of olives, cowries, and cones. One of these, we discover later, is an aulicus cone, and he is lucky to have escaped without a fatal sting from it.

"Where did you find those?"

"Only about three hundred yards out. You need only swim to that dark patch? That's where they are feeding."

As the water is glacial this program lacks appeal, so we hire instead a *pedalo,* a vessel in which the operators recline side by side in deck chairs, propelling the craft, as the name suggests, by means of pedals. The start of this expedition is propitious. The sun breaks through, and the Mountain of Morne, lopsided as ever, poor thing, looms like the prow of a sinking ship against a sky of a particularly lucid blue. The *pedalo* progresses on oiled ballbearings towards the objective which, however, seems to have disappeared. As we leave the shelter of the headland a slight marine disturbance modifies our progress, and we become aware of the boom of the reef. Pat girds himself for *la chasse,* with mask, spike, flippers, and gloves, and disappears overboard. His progress, in some current opposing that which is beginning to bear me toward the reef, is marked by his snorkle. I do not wish it to be thought that mine is a complaining nature, but at this moment an offshore gust of wind arises driving the *pedalo* before it like a fallen leaf. The *pedalo,* accustomed to two sets of two sets of pedals working equally, now describes a wide circle, demonstrating its preference for the reef. Even by the most violent exertion I am unable to maintain my status quo and progress, backwards and crabwise, towards certain doom. Pat emerges in the distance and gesticulates imperiously for me to approach.

"I can't manage the bloody boat," I bellow, gesticulating back with equal urgency, a whisper against the roar of the reef.

With a cheerful thumbs up sign, Pat submerges once more and moves evenly off in the opposite direction. At this moment the gust dies away as abruptly as it arose and by the exertion to their maximum of long disused muscles, I churn off after his retreating snorkle. The fruits of this expedition can be weighed only in terms of the experience bought with them. Namely, a *pedalo* is a vessel designed for millpond conditions, to be operated by two strong pairs of legs working in unison; also a gymnastic feat is needed to regain the vessel once you have left it. Furthermore, it is imprudent to make such an expedition without a flagon of sun oil, a parasol, and a distress rocket.

The guests in the hotel have all come prepared for a tropical sojourn, only to be reduced by the cold to wearing layers of summer clothing one on top of the other. Upset tummies and heavy colds are taken for granted. One drastic family has cut short their leave to fly home to England. We also begin to feel the need for a wind of change, but as it is unlikely to be warmer anywhere else within reach and cholera has broken out further east, the obvious alternative is to move to the other main hotel in the island, Le Chaland.

These plans have an unsettling effect upon the Maneeram family. Bobby and Jim both beseech Pat to take them back with him to England. But what on earth would they do there? Both discover a sudden vocation to train as nurses. Salted with brine, pared down by the wind, light on their feet as sea birds, it is hard to imagine two more unlikely candidates for the department of ministering angels, but they decline to be dissuaded. We suspect they have been tipped off that the home office is admitting any foreigners willing to work as male orderlies.

"We want to ask you to come to our house tonight to eat an Indian dinner with us," proposes Bobby tentatively one afternoon.

Wishing to do the occasion justice and also to strike the right note, we pay considerable attention to our clothing. Pat succeeds in dressing in exactly the same formula as our hosts, in a brightly colored shirt with white slacks. The Indian ladies will wear saris, I presume, since I have seen both Leila and her mother-in-law in them by day, so I wear a long-sleeved pink cotton dress with shell jewelry.

We are received by Jack and Bobby in the parlor with lights

ablaze and the windows wide open. The ceiling, in consequence, is black with mosquitoes. The room is decked with shells and branches, while the radio roars at full blast. The rest of the house is in darkness, silent but for the occasional light step of a bare foot and the sigh of simmering food. The table is laid for four.

Presently Bobby's mother enters laden with dishes, shielding her face with her sari. She shadows away in alarm when we rise to greet her. We catch a glimpse of her husband hovering nervously in the hallway.

"Did you say your parents live here, Bobby?"

"They sleep in the hut behind the house."

We both refrain from saying, "But you said the cow lived in that hut at the back." Indeed, this morning we saw Bobby's mother in attendance upon this cow, tottering up the path and into the hut, a huge sheaf on her head destined for its sacred luncheon.

Leila now enters with an iron pot of stew made from the fish we caught this morning on the reef plus bowls of red and grccn peppers, onions, herbs, and curry. This is accompanied by a fiery chutney and by fried chapatis, a sort of unleavened bread eaten with the curry with a view to modifying its fury. All this is washed down by rum mixed with coconut milk. I take a sip which makes me blink, followed by a mouthful of stew which promotes a gush of tears and a spear thrust in the throat. By necessity an exponent of the bland food school of cooking, I might as well be eating prussic acid. Fortunately, the menu is relished by Pat, who, with occasional outbreaks of tears, polishes off his share, which ends with a selection of fruits from the garden, including papaya, mango, jackfruit, lemons, and pineapple.

The conversation centers round two distaff spindle shells, which Bobby says are always found in conjugal pairs, and a specimen of the violet spider conch shell, the wonderful *Lambis violacea*, which he ran to earth in Port Louis and for which Pat pays him 400 rupees, or about £30. This is a princess among shells, the lip and every finger in mint condition, radiant in its silky sheen, its orifice stained a deep purple, as if with the

A specimen of the rare violet spider conch (*Lambis violacea*).
Photograph by Sara Heaton.

royal dye of ancient Phoenicia. In fact, so mint was its condition that under its operculum were two entire whelks, pickled in formaldehyde. Actually, I already own one, for which I paid a mere 200 rupees, which, lacking gloss and inferior in color, also has a chip on its shoulder.

Bobby's sole comment on my acquisition was:

"I told you to wait."

When we leave, Bobby proudly hands us his new business card. It reads: "For your problem of seashells collections and boats for tours on sea-place contact Mr. Bobby."

He scans our guarded expressions anxiously.

"It's no good?" he inquires astutely. "Tell me. Perhaps I put it next time."

"Boat, with guide, for reef shelling. Shells cleaned. Rare shells for sale." We suggest tentatively after consultation.

Bobby looks nettled and tucks the card away in silence. He hates to be found wanting but never fails to take a point.

On the evening we are due at Le Chaland, the weather relents and within the hour turns from midwinter to full summer. The sea is dappled violet and aquamarine, the sky a cloudless dome, the sun a benediction without venom or sting. Whether the fingerposts directing us to Le Chaland, which adjoins the airport, are at fault, or whether we miss a turning through being engrossed in discussion I do not know, but soon we are gliding comfortably along an air strip, surrounded on all sides by quivering fields of sugar cane.

"What's the time?"

"About four o'clock."

"The BOAC plane is just about due."

I haven't felt so exposed since the family bathing tent blew away leaving me naked on the beach in Dumpton Gap. It's like trying to find the way out of a mangrove swamp. We nose along the edge searching for a means of escape and presently find one marked No Exit, a prohibition we naturally ignore.

Le Chaland is a cosy thatched establishment presided over by a Mr. Harry Hargreaves, the worse for a monumental black eye, who greets us in the company of the first well-bred dog we have met on the island, a disdainful alsatian with a proudly uplifted brush.

"I could easily stay here a month," remarks Pat as we settle into a bedroom overlooking an apocalyptic sunset like a late Turner painting, and a foam of flowering bushes. Nevertheless, his backward-glancing comment as we take off for the island of Rèunion a week later is, "One more day on that island and I think I would have gone berserk."

A month or so after our return we receive the following communication from Bobby: "Friendship is the flower that bloom in all season. I wish it may grow ever green in your garden." Here follows a spirited sketch of a forget-me-not. Soon, he concludes, he too will marry, after all. (If not, his friend will pinch his girl.) Will Pat please lend him many rupees to build a bungalow and buy a boat?

9 Bali

Pat has descended upon Beirut without so much as pinpointing it on the map, and might be anywhere. He has become aware, however, from the Arabic flavor of our surroundings that we have not yet attained Bali, our ultimate destination. I have the advantage of him, having visited the Lebanon before the last war, when Beirut was a moldering Phoenician port, a city still dreaming of the cedars of Lebanon, of the tears of Isis, of the clash of crusading arms, and of the imperial purple dye extracted from the murex shells that proliferated in the shallows. But these memories are no guide to the Beirut of the 1970s, which is now composed of concrete cliffs of apartment houses and glittering hotels, of labyrinthine streets clanging with the honk of impatient cars, and crammed with half of the entire Lebanese population.

Disquiet prevails. The murmuring in the cafés is of hijacking, of Black September, of inevitable war, and of the rocketing cost of living. No scholarly appraisal of the archaic scene is possible, for we have both neglected to do any preliminary homework. Pat, having decided that mythology gives him the willies and Egyptian pharoahs the creeps, is nevertheless predisposed to listen to a well-prepared resumé of facts, in the innocent expectation that I, by way of being on the executive of a Central Asian school of archaeology, am an expert on the Giblites, on Ibshimu, Astargates, and other such.

"There's nowhere called Phoenicia on this ancient map. What happened to it?"

"Alas, poor Phishes! Cut into strips and swallowed whole when they lost the war."

"Yes, but which war?"

"Whatever war it was. The one against Cyrus the Great, probably, or Sennacherib . . . or . . . er . . . Alexander the Great."

"I'd like my money back, please. I don't believe you know any more about it than I do."

Drivers of cars here use a technique acquired in the unrestricted space of a desert like one huge hard tennis court, and may the worst brakes lose. No ill-feeling is engendered among them, however, as they dart, thrust, zoom, and weave about like mayflies, but a toll is taken of the nerves of any passenger who wishes primarily to live and only secondarily to reach Baalbek, say, or Byblos, known more graphically in its fourth millenium as Giblet. These two ancient cities have been vividly described by others, but none that I know of has done justice to Josef, our driver, through whom alone we survived these expeditions. A circular fleece headdress sits low on his brow from under which squint disillusioned black eyes. A broken nose swerves left above impeccably waxed moustaches like handlebars. His hands are lean and clean, delicate as a musician's, and his least utterance has an engraved quality. Once, it seems, he possessed his own cab, but when his wife got T.B. he sold it to send her to Davos, where she died just the same. Now Josef drives for the Mafia-type syndicate that operates like an iron mesh across the threshold of our hotel, extending even to the gold market, where we note we are being somewhat oafishly shadowed.

Not for Josef, fortunately, the electric-eel tactics of the Lebanese charioteer. "Let him go!" he remarks urbanely as a lorry cuts in with blaring horn, almost landing us in a ditch. "We are not here for the races, but to see the sun on the snowy mountains" (the Israeli Army is established among the peaks), "the apple blossom on the terraces, and this plain, Monsieur, on which once walked Jesus Christ himself."

Bangkok is the next stop, and here also the air is charged with tension. Inside the customs shed both the coming-forth

Surrounded by rushing brooks, lily ponds, flower-burdened trees, brilliant birds, and monkeys. Bangkok, Thailand. Photograph by Patrick Hodgson.

and the entering-in are intimately searched for time bombs and hand grenades. With the thermometer standing at over a hundred we roar in low gear through the maelstrom of Bangkok. At its present rate of development, there will soon be nothing left for tourists to see except the high-rise hotels built to accommodate them. Our driver is in somber spirits. Fighting is in progress three hundred miles away, and who knows when and where it will spread? Unemployment is rife; the young can get jobs in the new hotels, but the old must also eat. His wife has bolted with a G.I., taking his son with her. Ministers of the Crown are misappropriating funds and appointing their relatives to key posts. Prices are soaring. The weather forecast is gloomy, and we too are understandably glum by the time we arrive. Composure, however, is restored by the charm of the hotel which stands within a royal park, surrounded by rushing brooks, lily ponds, flower-burdened trees, brilliant birds, monkeys, and a tame duck, Edwin. Uttering periodic duck comments, Edwin plods methodically behind us to our garden-level bedroom where, with apologies, I shut the glass door in his face. He is outraged. "Quack, quack!" he bawls, ruffling his feathers, rotating his tail and rapping sharply on

Nearly a week streams past in a procession of palaces, temples, and monasteries, among pagodas, monuments, and Buddhas, emerald, golden, and bronze. Bangkok, Thailand. Photograph by Patrick Hodgson.

"We need peace in which to meditate," said the young man gently.
Bangkok, Thailand. Photograph by Patrick Hodgson.

the window pane with his beak. "Quack!" I reply crisply, tapping back from inside. "Quack to you," he retorts, pausing to unload himself on the step before withdrawing in dudgeon to the swimming pool, where he is next seen rocking upon its pellucid surface, gently nibbling at passing swimmers.

Nearly a week streams past in a procession of palaces, temples, and monastries, among pagodas, monuments, and Buddhas, emerald, golden, and bronze. We are guided by students, or by saffron-robed monks, amid a people remarkable for their fine-boned beauty and distinction, who manifest daily the Buddist virtues of serenity, loving kindness, and resigned commonsense, and if an ironic gleam lurks in their dispassionate gaze, it is sometimes hardly surprising.

"Why do you still build temples when those you already have are empty?" It is midnight in the Chao Phraya bar, which divides Pat perched on a stool from the philosopher serving drinks behind it.

"We need peace in which to meditate," replies the young man gently. "Each wishes, therefore, to be alone in the temple; thus we build many." By the time Pat retires for the night he is the richer by the four Great Truths and the Noble Eightfold Way of Guatama the Buddha, the Enlightened One. Over 90 percent of Thailand is Buddist, and most young men, this barman included, spend several years in the priesthood before embarking on their secular career.

Several times sunrise finds us in the fascinating Klong river market, where once farmers paddled their cornucopian canoes, laden down to the waterline with fruit and vegetables. Progress has now introduced a bedlam of motor vessels, which a policeman with a megaphone directs from the roof of a patrol boat. At moonrise the temple dancers weave their way across the courtyard of our hotel, glistening in gold brocade and with headdresses like miniature pagodas. The knee is bent, the lifted foot is heel down, toe up, while the hands, backcurved with three-inch golden fingernails, twist sinuously to the soft jangle of the xylophone, the one-stringed fiddle and to muted bells.

"Their hands look like Thai Spider conch shells," whispers Pat as he glimpses them silhouetted against the torchlight.

The fascinating Klong river market. Bangkok. Photograph by Patrick Hodgson.

Indeed I have often noticed the correspondence between the mollusk and the environment from which it draws life. The cockleshells of Spain, for instance, look like ruffled skirts, and the pectens like black fans. The Mexican limpet is a sombrero in miniature, the starfish a somber Aztec sunburst, and the shells assume the colors of the soil—burnt sienna, blood red, or sable-dark. In Bali the limpet is the coolie hat worn in the rice paddies; the Pagoda periwinkle is the image of a Batur temple. Certain Japanese shells curve upward like the eaves of a Kyoto temple, while the *Cypraea mauritiana,* found off Tanzania, is a polished Negro bronze. The ashen shades of British mollusks remind me perpetually of mackintoshes.

We now stall for ten days amidst the legendary arcades and treasure houses of Hong Kong. For centuries the Chinese have regarded all foreigners with contempt, confident, it would seem, in their own superiority as the cradle of culture and of right thinking. Around 1848, it dawned upon the mandarins that the unprincipled British were dishing out opium from India to the Chinese, who were cheerfully demoralizing themselves with it. Peking suddenly got tough and, beseiging some sacred British warehouses, confiscated a substantial consignment. The prime minister, Lord Palmerston, was quite put out, and instantly demanded a refund of its total value. This precipitated the so-called Opium War, which ended with the Chinese paying compensation for the drugs (already at the bottom of the China Sea) and with the cession of Hong Kong to the British on a long lease as a penance for their folly. Glittering in the bay like New York transported, it still more or less appertains to Britain, at least until the lease runs out in 1990, or until Mao Tse-Tung decides otherwise.

With what immaculate taste the Chinese are endowed! It is not just one object in one shop for which the heart craves, or even several in several shops, but almost everything in every shop. Painting, jade, gems, furniture, ivories, silver, crystal, ceramics, furs, embroidery, brocades, carpets, handbags, luggage, cameras, tape recorders, radios, watches. The effect is paralyzing. Every treasure is almost certain to be surpassed in beauty and value around the corner in the next arcade.

The choice is so overwhelming that it promotes disability; after a week I sink into bed on a diet of boiled fish.

Combing the back streets and bazaars in search of chinoiserie, with which to embellish a bird's nest of a flat overhanging the fluted columns of Regency Square and the doomed west pier of Brighton, we presently drift through the portals of the Chinese Emporium. Here almost everything we have been seeking seems to be assembled under one roof.

"May I see that table, please?"

"Well, look at it!"

I am stupified. ("Abroad is bloody," said Nancy Mitford's Uncle Matthew with some truth, "and all foreigners are fiends.")

"But there are others on top of it." Silence.

"Tell me, do you expect me to buy that table without being able to see it?"

Scowl; crash; bang. What's gone wrong? Normally any such request here is met with a warm response, good-natured bartering, and laughter. Eventually we buy this table—I am typing on it at this moment—and much else besides, in an atmosphere about as breezy as a swamp before the monsoon breaks. Only when confronted by the manager, invested with a scarlet Maoist plaque, do we realize we are dealing with the Red China government shop. Whilst he is settling the account, Pat is presented with the little red book, *The Sayings of Mao Tse-tung,* and subjected to a harangue, the gist of which is that only the Chinese desire peace; an opinion which Pat is unable to share, and he says so. Unlikely though it seems, this exchange ends up on a harmonious note. Down the side of the bill the manager inscribes some Chinese characters in an exquisite hand.

"What does that say?"

"I write your name in Chinese. See? Cyprus Tree, Virtue, Strength, Labor, Guest, Officer of Queen."

On our last visit to Bali, by ship, the *Caronia* anchored off some rice paddies under the shadow of the great volcano, Gungung Agang, which immediately manifested uncomplimentary symptoms of protest. A few passengers hired taxis and in suffocating heat drove into the capital, Denpasar, which, it was reported, they held in low regard. The rest made sallies on shore under a continuous rain of fine black ash, to buy or to barter for Balinese works of art, retreating frequently to the air-conditioned ship for iced Coca-Cola. Pat and I, as usual, passed the time combing the scalding beaches from which we acquired a modest assembly of shells. As the ship sailed away, at sundown on the third day, we saw the top of the volcano blow off with a hellish red glare and an ear-splitting explosion. Although several miles out to sea the *Caronia* was smothered in black dust. We never knew why we did not put back to help. Later we heard that the Balinese, believing the gods to be righteously incensed at their wickedness, decked themselves with flowers and threw themselves in the path of the boiling lava, offering up their lives in an ecstacy of humility and expiation. The death roll at "the navel of the world" exceeded ten thousand.

Since then a highrise hotel, the Bali Beach, has incongruously appeared on the shore at Senur, close both to the airport and to Denpasar. Radical changes in the political scene have not altered the Balinese conviction that Bali is the centre of the universe. True, they have become aware of other islands in the archipelago and have even registered the existence of greater islands still, known as continents, but these shadowy entities have about as much reality to the Balinese as hell has to the modern American.

The universe then, some ninety miles long, lies off the coast of Java upon a girdle of rock from which three hundred volcanoes tower above the sea. Except for a visit by Marco Polo in 1292, the island was left in total isolation until its conquest by the Dutch in the early twentieth century, a fantastic world of kingly courts, magic cults, sacred volcanoes, festivals, and ritual. Nature was so bountiful that toil was a rare necessity, leaving the islanders endless leisure in which to propitiate the benign power of Tengon and the deadly forces of Kiwa; to engage, in fact, in the full-time job of maintaining a balance between absolute good and absolute evil.

It is compulsory before attaining this "earthly paradise" to be punctured against a variety of tropical diseases, and prudent

As the *Caronia* sailed away, we saw the top of the volcano, Gungung Agang, blow off with a hellish red glare and an ear-splitting explosion. Bali. Photograph by Patrick Hodgson.

to swallow daily a remedy against malaria. A thriving surgery near the swimming pool has prescribed capsules against last week's Hong Kong tummy, antibiotics against this week's Bali tummy, vitamins to counteract the antibiotics, and entrovioform to prevent everything else. Topped up by a daily dose to disinfect and salt tablets to offset the heat, the passing scene is gradually becoming hazy at the edges. Meanwhile, the waiting room is swarming with customers from Cheltenham, Melbourne, or Philadelphia, with constitutions hitherto untested by Cantonese cooking and Bali bugs. Those wayfarers who have avoided digestive problems are struggling with heavy colds, since the thermometer on the terrace stands at well over a 100 degrees while the marble halls inside are kept at the temperature of a crisp October morning in New York.

Njepi is upon us, the Balinese New Year, the date of which is linked to the spring equinox. On the eve of this festival the population strenuously exorcises the sins committed during the year that is dying. At every crossroad fruits of the earth and small trussed animals are piled high, over which presides a

Squawking birds, chaplets of flowers, and cunningly contrived baskets of fruit are cast as sacrifices upon the water. Photograph by Douglas Dickins.

loudly praying priest. Fantastic deities, sheltered under sacred umbrellas, are borne aloft from the temple down to the shore, accompanied by a riot of mask-dancing, frenzied chanting, clashing of gongs, and violently gesticulating priests. Squawking birds, chaplets of flowers, and cunningly contrived baskets of fruit are cast as sacrifices upon the water with incantation and mime. It is impossible to know whether we are participating in the equivalent of Mardi Gras or in a solemn act of worship. We play it safe, wearing ceremonial sashes and respectful expressions, and mingle tentatively with the enraptured throng.

The next day is celebrated by a resolute silence. No lights or fires are kindled, no work accomplished, no footfall disturbs the deserted streets. All are given over to fasting, prayer, and meditation. As a result, a partial paralysis overcomes the hotel which, sustained by yesterday's food, totters on supported by a skeleton staff of Moslems, Chinese, and one Methodist.

We join in the universal mood and retire into a thatched hut on the beach with our history books in the hope of finding out what is going on. These transport us back into medieval times, when the Hindu princes of Java, fleeing from the power of Islam, found sanctuary in the courts of Bali, bringing with them retinues of priests, poets, painters, and philosophers. They also introduced into Bali their caste system and the complex language of the courtesies associated with it. Social intercourse thereafter developed into one everlasting pitfall. The newly appointed manager of the hotel, for instance, complained distractedly to Pat that among his staff of twelve hundred (who serve six hundred guests), only to five may he issue any direct order or make any personal request. Each retainer disdainfully delegates to the man below until the appropriate level is found.

During the sixteenth century Dutch traders moved into Indonesia, where they eventually formed the Dutch East Indies. The Balinese were included in them geographically, but in no other sense. For three centuries the ruling caste, the *satria*, totally ignored the existence of the detested intruders, but in 1906 a showdown occurred that resulted in their extinction. I hope it was some consolation that their closing scene was enacted with faultless showmanship.

As a reprisal for some trifling incident, several Dutch men-of-war threatened the coast and were harried in return by a Balinese force armed with golden spears. The outraged Dutch retaliated by bombarding Denpasar from their ships, followed by an assault on the city with troops and cannon. The civilian population sensibly melted away into the landscape, while the *radja* hastily mustered a train of princes, princesses, nobles, generals, musicians, and scholars. Adorned in cloth of gold and loaded with gems, but armed only with golden krises, they emerged together from the ruins of their flaming palaces straight into the Dutch rifle fire. A neighboring prince rushed to their support but was captured and instantly slit his own throat. Led by the *radja* and fighting to the death against impossible odds, the entire *satria* proceeded to commit mass suicide. The moon rose upon a cairn of mutilated warriors and women who, their regalia blackened with blood, had crawled together to overlie the body of their slaughtered king. Since then, the Japanese have passed like locusts over Bali in World War II, a renewal of Dutch colonial rule has been bloodily repulsed, and a constitutional government of Indonesia has been intermittently established. But these events, like the life at the courts of the kings of Bali, have never penetrated deeply into the rice paddies, and life flows on undisturbed in the village, the temple, and under the banyan tree.

In the meantime the Indonesian Ocean celebrates *njepi* in dramatic fashion by withdrawing almost from view, exposing ridges of dying reef like decayed teeth. Interspersed between them are expanses of emerald weed, transforming the mud flats into one endless aquatic billiard table. At high tide the sea ignores all regulations by dashing itself against the expensive hotel terrace, throwing up walls of disrespectful water.

We take advantage of the ebb tide to explore the reef without being inconvenienced by the presence of the sea. It is in poor shape. The coral has been hacked away by the villagers to reinforce their roads and shore up their houses; what remains is liable to collapse under our weight into underlying pools, which smell potently of sewage. Shoals of cheerfully hued fish, however, wag their way about on their lawful occasions. Only a rather limited range of beaten-up shells are disclosed, all but one of which we already possess—an orange-mouthed olive, a gleaming brunette with curved vermilion lips.

A troop of polite children attends our search close in to heel. "Welcome to Ba-li. Where you came from? What is your name? You want to buy carving, batik, painting?" When it penetrates that what we actually want is seashells, which anyone can cull free on the reef, we are almost smothered in goodwill. Children materialize instantly from all quarters, laden with candy-striped land snails, turrets, latiaxis, dials, nautiluses from the fishing nets and, of course, our old chum the tiger cowry, dwarfed here, even when full grown, and oddly humped. Cowries, incidentally, among those mollusks that are hermaphroditic or prone to changes of sex. They mate zestfully and the female even sits on her eggs, although her aim is not to hatch them out but to protect them from predators.

"Look, Mister Pat! Two olives! Two hundred rupiahs!"

"I'll give you twenty for three."

"Okay." And off they bound, radiant with success.

As elsewhere, our eyes serve us less keenly than those compelled to comb the rocks for their daily fare, but well enough to restore a familiar ambience to bathroom and balcony; a whiff of elderly fish, cairns of shells on a platter pinched off the breakfast tray, a wash basin permanently choked with sand. Our passion cools somewhat as researches reveal that no sovereign shell reigns in Bali as in, for instance, Fiji, Mauritius, Florida, or Mexico; that the moon is at an adverse angle; that conditions are arduous and the prospect of an enlightened guide a pipe dream. Also squids have been washed up on the beach, seventy-five feet long. So we find ourselves drawn imperceptibly towards other attractions that both bewilder and fascinate.

I have earlier lamented the destruction of the cultures that were enjoyed by islands such as Tahiti and the Hawaiian group (missionaries on the menu precludes Fiji from the list) before the traders, the whalers, and the do-gooders accomplished their aims. On Bali, however, primeval innocence has not yet been extinguished. Its inhabitants are single minded in a total commitment to religious observance, which lasts from birth to death and into the hereafter. Centered on the village temple, their religion orders every aspect of their daily·life, enriches it with continual artistic expression and permeates it with joy, affection, and a sense of oneness with the forces of nature. One omnipotent God presides over a universe stretched between the two poles of good and evil, from the sky beyond the hallowed volcanoes, to the ferocious deeps of the inimical sea. (No wonder we cannot get a guide.) Human beings exist in an intermediary sphere, honoring the benevolent deities above, placating the infernal spirits below. These lesser deities, both benign and hostile, are but different manifestations of the Great One, the Holy One, the Supreme God of All —Sanghyang Widi.

Fifty thousand temples and shrines are said to thrive in Bali, an island comparable in size to the state of Delaware. We do not contemplate visiting them all, hoping that an exploration of a few will be enough to induce an understanding heart. Every village or desa, possesses at least three —one used for official ceremonies, one for ancestor worship and the third for the all absorbing rites which surround death.

The desa consists of rows of compounds clustered round a central square, where flourish the temples, the market, the cockfighting pit, the bell tower, and the sacred tree of the Hindu, the banyan, our old friend whose seed will grow only when passed through a bird. The priest, identifiable by his white robe, is alone entitled to wear a beard. As a result, some confusion has arisen from an eruption of particularly hirsute hippies from the mid-week plane, clad in undeniably white, but particularly unpriestly denims and sweat shirts.

We slice through a group of these intruders as we tear along the road towards the water temple of Mengwi, leaving a scattered wake of children, bearers of wood and water, hogs, goats, and cocks leaping for their lives. Glimpses stream past of women beating their sarongs on the flat stones of a river, or threshing rice in a compound; of naked tottering infants; of men in limpetlike hats, serviceable as either umbrella or sunshade. "Slower," bellows Pat poking the driver in the back. With a radiant smile he swivels round in his seat and mounts the verge grazing the bark off a breadfruit tree. "Goodnight!" is his unnerving reply, after which he recovers

We tear along the road towards the water temple of Mengwi. Bali.
Photograph by Patrick Hodgson.

momentum and continues, as if competing in the Grand Prix.
We can only commit our lives to the stone gods stationed at
every crossroad, wearing, for some reason connected with
njepi, black and white aprons over their private parts. Explo-
sions of rain alternate with bursts of sunshine as we ascend
between terraces of rippling chartreuse green rice paddies,
pricked through with votive temples to attract a heavenly
benediction upon the crops.

The moated temple of Mengwi is in a somewhat uncertain
state of repair. Like many others, it is left unoccupied except
on such holy days as the anniversary of its foundation, when
the gods descend to earth for a junket. The faithful, in full
fig, then entertain their sacred visitors and one another, with
revels and dancing, masques and masquerades, feasting and
libation. The entrance, which consists of a split gateway like
the two halves of a bisected tower, sags a little under an access

of dragons. Within, two open courtyards adjoin one another, where little upkeep is called for and little given, beyond some rudimentary lawnmowing. The outer court is the antechamber to the inner and more sacred enclosure, which is guarded by a pair of scowling stone giants. To one of these is secured a noticeboard which reads:

"Attention! Ladies during menstruation are requested not to enter this temple."

"Menstruating ladies impure," explains a guide genially who has attached himself to our retinue of children and chickens. Behind his ear he wears a hibiscus, indicating that his day's devotions have been performed.

"I suppose this is where the priest presides?," I enquire in a reverent undertone, indicating a thatched pavilion to the right.

"Cockfighting pit," he replies cheerfully.

Pat, who saw conflicts to the death last week, says that each cock has a cutthroat steel spur strapped to one leg and that the first slash usually decides the contest. The bookie, known as the Kristo because his stance resembles a crucifix, accepts a deluge of bets with a flick of a glance for each, and has never been known to make a mistake.

"In this pavilion," continues the guide, "people lay offerings. Yonder twinks gamelan orchestra—bamboo flute, drums, gongs —pom-pom, ting-ting." (We know all too well.) "Here, priests sprinkle people with holy water. Here, dancing. These pagodas —see?—one for each holy mountain. Here, three altars to Holy Trinity—Wind, Fire, Water."

"Water?" I am startled, for the sea is held in such super-stitious terror by the Balinese that few dare to fish in the teeming bays or have even learned to swim.

"To the holy mountain the faithful lift up their eyes," the guide explains, lifting up his own. "By streams of living water are they purified, or by rivers of burning lava are they consumed."

The pattern of modern travel is gradually imposing itself upon our consciousness. Busloads of perspiring tourists file continuously through the hotel lobby and, three days later, surfeited with temple-dancing, holy mountains, cockfighting, paintings from Ubad, and wood carvings from Mas, they file out again. With the tour leader setting a relentlessly matey example, each group has eaten communely at one table, slumbered in adjacent bedrooms and, ever together, it roves onward to identical stints at five more tourist centers. No member of the party is ever beyond the reach of a blue rinse, a Coca-Cola, a nice cup of tea, a hamburger, or an ice cube. The very air they are breathing is implicit with magic, monsters, and witches. Panthers and tigers prowl the mountainside under wheeling stars, while crocodiles sigh and stir in the swamps. Do these birds of passage, I wonder, ever find time to step alone into the darkness, to listen to the systole and diastole of the heartbeat of the stealthy and spirit-laden night?

Amid the general ebb and flow, we join forces in the Baris bar with the only other static couple, a Tanzanian diplomat and his wife. The velvety darkness is relieved only by an occasional candle. Our host, wearing a bible-black city suit, has established himself upon a dark sofa that provides so perfect a camouflage that I sit down squarely on his lap. "Good gracious, I didn't see you!" I exclaim somewhat superfluously as the gloom is split by two crescent-shaped smiles of welcome.

A crisp young German, Renate Wittig, who presides over the female staff of the hotel, also gropes her way in to join us. Somehow or other she has succeeded in transforming several hundred Hindus, accustomed to living on the earth in bamboo shacks, into neat bedmakers, dazzling polishers, and nonchalant handlers of Hoovers, air-conditioners and intercom. Among her other preoccupations are numbered horse raising, orchid growing, photography—yes, and shell collecting! A few hundred yards along the shore she has built a shell museum, encompassed by a garden asway with amethyst, aureate, and freckled orchids. Renate, with a Balinese student, Agus, who acts as curator of her museum, have spent the last few years in combing the coastline, as well as most of the offshore islands. The most fruitful reef, she says, is several hours away to the north, inaccessible except at certain phases of the moon; another is near our anchorage of eight years ago where we gathered our first modest harvest of Balinese shells. By sleeping on the beach and rising at dawn to dive for them when the tide was right, they have assembled an array of some thousands of shells —most of them, of course, many times duplicated—in immaculate condition. One vitrine is devoted entirely to cowries. All are scientifically labelled and stylishly displayed in tiers of black-lined vitrines, or stashed away in ancient Cantonese coffers inlaid with abalone shells. These chests were used originally to store consignments of coins, called *pipis bolong*, which were sent to Bali by Chinese merchants of the Ming dynasty for the simplification of trade.

From about 2000 B.C. money cowries (*Cypraea moneta*) had been in use as currency in China, but these gave way first to cowry-shaped metal coins and subsequently to coin as we now know it. The son of heaven (the Chinese emperor) on his death was traditionally entombed with nine such cowries in his mouth. (The present Japanese emperor, incidentally, owns one of the finest shell collections in the world.) Egyptian mummies were often given cowries for eyes to ensure good eyesight in the hereafter. The all-seeing eyes of idols in certain parts of Africa frequently consisted of cowries with the aperture turned outwards. Drumsticks made from human bones were often studded with money cowries, which were also widely used as exchange in the slave traffic. These same cowries are quite common in British collections, for a ship from the Philippines with a cargo of them capsized off the Cumbrian coast at the end of the last century, and they were washed up on our beaches in their thousands.

As we leave the museum we fall into step with a stately old woman who presently invites us into her house, which stands back from the water in a Stygian-like grove. She turns out to be Bali's most famous legong dancer, Ni Polok, no less, who at the peak of her fame married a middle-aged Belgian artist and became his sole model until his death thirty years later. M. Le Mayer's paintings have faded in the blinding light and are now disintegrating in the damp, but we can still see that they are all variations of the same theme; a legong dancer with lustrous ropes of blue-black hair and somber wide-set eyes.

Any passing pedestrian can tell the traveler where and when a celebration is about to occur, since he can instantly recognize

The Legong dance, usually performed by two young girls. Bali.

and pinpoint local outbreaks of ceremonial dress. It is by such means that we happen upon a performance of the *ketjak* dance, enacted in the cockpit of a village, with an unpronounceable name, perhaps twenty miles from the simple skyscraper we call home. Some two hundred men, clad only in loin cloths, are crouching in concentric circles around a branching torch. The silence is broken only by an occasional soft hissing, and by the swaying of glistening torsos. A gradual crescendo of a bass chant is suddenly pierced by one spine-chilling yell, followed by the fluttering of hundreds of sable hands. When the dance ends it is by a dramatic backward fall with outflung arms, like the explosive flowering of some huge bud. The aim of this unnerving and erotic performance is exorcism; in effect, it is highly cathartic and not only, perhaps, for the participants.

Occasional displays of classical dancing occur in the garden restaurant of the hotel, supported by our village gamelan orchestra, who rate in the island as the equivalent of the top of the pops. The accompaniment ranges from the clink of metallophones and a wail of woodreed so subtle that the music seems to originate in the mind, to the ear-splitting roll of differently strung drums and clashing gongs. Illuminated by torchlight, reincarnations from the ancient courts of Bali glide across the arena, elegant, intent, formalized. The dancers are swathed in brocade and flashing with gems, their weapons are of gold and their hair threaded through with flowers, while the perfumed air is stirred only by the flourish of silk fans or by floating scarves. To concentrate on this vivid prospect and at the same time make a prudent choice from the menu imposes a severe strain on the spectator. "What is this you have brought me, Siadja?"

"*Saté*, njonja."

"*Saté?*" I examine the menu through lorgnettes, bought in Hong Kong for menu examining, but which distort the vision. If *saté* is to be my fate it will not only be the vision that is distorted. "Saté" I read "iss screwed chunk of goat meat, girled chaps, pil cod fisils, slopped in soy sauce, stir fried in garlic, pippers and lime squashed."

"Haven't you got anything else?"

"Leicester lamb, njonja." Nostalgia grips me. At least I think

207

The aim of this explosive and unnerving performance is exorcism; it is in effect highly cathartic and not only, perhaps, for the participants. The *Ketjak* dance. Bali. Photograph courtesy of FotoKeinpen.

it is nostalgia. What could be safer? No other animal, Mrs. Beeton declared roundly in 1861, possesses the power of converting pasture into flesh in so remarkable a degree as the Leicestershire sheep. So lamb it is, succeeded by Jello de jour, but all this vigilance goes for nought, because I get hepatitis later anyway and might just as well have enjoyed the screwed goat.

Meanwhile, into the floodlit arena against a backdrop of
black ocean, a supple male figure has appeared, glimmering
with jewels and crowned with trembling translucent quills that
seem to assume a life of their own, like a sprung diamond rose
on a tiara. Preoccupied by gastronomic problems and hypnotized
by the vibrating headdress, the quality of his performance at
first escapes me.

"I don't know whether this fellow is a man or a boy," whispers Pat, "but he sure can dance." With fork suspended I focus my wandering attention upon him. Wild as a bird, light as the wind, with a tender mobility of feature, and with hands like wings, this youth emanates a steady ray of distinction and magnetism.

> O body swayed to music, O brightening glance,
> How can we know the dancer from the dance?

Even if one had never before seen star quality, it would be impossible not to recognize it now. He is performing the traditional baris dance, in which the warrior dedicates himself to victory or to death, expressing both compassion for his victims and ruthlessness towards his foes. I am instantly transported back to my eighth birthday when, in "The Spectre of the Rose," Nijinsky soared from the wings to remain momentarily carved upon the air in an unforgettable attitude of grace and power. I trained for the ballet until I was twelve as the result of that leap.

At the end of the dance I rush upstairs and pick out a gilt fountain pen from a treasure trove bought in London against such a contingency. This I send to the warrior with a letter of acclaim. Just in time I remember that in Bali it is a courtesy, when giving a present, to leave on the price tag. The father of the dancer appears like an arrow in a state of exaltation. Tonight is the debut of his son, Ngurah Harimbhawa, who has been schooled from infancy by his great-uncle, the supreme master of the baris. The old man himself, Ib Sanskanbun, can be seen lurking in the shadow of a moss-covered wall, looking like a fresco in some disintegrating temple.

The following morning finds me attending the daily dance session in the family compound in Senur. The father, Nura Madja, patters with his fingertips on an elongated drum as an accompaniment. The youth, beautiful as a golden hind, is treated to twenty minutes of hell by Ib, that aged perfectionist, whose hooded black eyes remain fixed upon a point above my head, as if concentrating upon some transcendental vision there. Lithe as a cobra, he sways behind his nephew, jerking up the

Ib Sanskanbun with his great-nephew Ngurah, jerking up the boy's chin, twisting arms. Bali. Photograph by Martha Hodgson.

boy's chin, twisting the arms, accentuating the angle of the hand, the curve of the finger. Nevertheless, while Ib is nearly wrenching off his pupil's arm, an almost tangible ray of tenderness and pride flows between the two performers.

"Ngurah seems very devoted to his uncle," I murmur into the father's ear.

Nura nods indulgently. "That is so," he whispers gently. "You can see, can you not, that there's no love lost between them?"

At this point a diminutive naked girl strolls into the room closely attended by a black piglet, its pendulous stomach bouncing on the floor. The session is over. The yard is thickly populated by Nura Madja's wife, her five younger moppets, lesser kith, and a throng of poultry and livestock, including a rackety fighting cock. Through the gate files an orderly line of buff ducks, tended by a patriarch bearing a crook and a long flexible bamboo with a frolic of feathers attached to the end. Over the compound wall rise the pagodas of the family temple, laden with the days offering of flowers, sweet cake, and *pipis bolong.*

Presently Nura Madja produces the stunning headdress worn the previous night by his son. It is made from long strips of the pearly *Nautilus pompilius,* a member of the octopus and squid fraternity, which are attached to the crown by a series of complex springs that cause them to tremble like wheat ears in the wind. The secret of this particular skill has apparently always been the monopoly of a single family. All the costumes are owned by the community, and fees earned by the dancers go into a kitty to pay for them. Before each performance, a priest sprinkles holy water over both costume and wearer and purifies the dancer by tracing mystic symbols on brow and limbs with the stem of a flower.

Pity the plight of any zealous missionary dished out with the task of converting these idolators to Christianity! For a start, the Balinese have no idols, for their temples and holy symbols are forever collapsing after each volcanic tremor or downpour of rain. The sole stone available in Bali is of a particularly crumbly nature, so that every statue, fresco, and carving has continually to be renewed. The effect of this is to maintain Balinese art as a living experience that grows and changes. Secondly, the form of Hinduism practiced here permeates not only the heart but the hearth, and an attempt to replace it by anything new would produce immediate social disintegration. Besides how could they improve on what they already have? "More than a religion," wrote the late Miguel Covarrubias in his memorable account of Bali, "it is a moral philosophy of high spiritual value, gay and free of fanaticism."

Such missionaries as have succeeded in establishing themselves at all have frequently withdrawn discomfited, leaving behind a residue of somewhat wayward converts.

"Why are you a Christian?" one of these star turns is reported by Mr. Covarrubias to have been asked.

Answer: "Because I believe."

"What do you believe?"

"I believe in Jesus Christ."

"And who is Jesus Christ?"

Silence. "I believe . . . er . . . he is the man in the dark suit who comes over in the ferry every Wednesday from Lombock."

Poor Bali! No longer "lovely and lost and half the world away." What hope is there for them when American hippies in their dozens are already lounging under the banyan trees?

What are they doing here? "Buying pictures, Ma'am," replies one. "Bali paintings are going big back home just now. And say, I can get high here for the price of a Coke in Arkansas, and the dolls are real cute. I sure dig their life-style. It's great!"

It seems a pity their life-style can't stay the way it is. Not only is it gentle, peaceful, productive, and good, but a socialistic life actually works here, being a community life in its purist sense. But above all they seem happy. Yet it is obviously impossible to continue to deny the Balinese the so-called benefits of the western media of communication, of education, and of medicine even if, at the same time, the doors are opened to Western standards, diseases, and drugs. They cannot remain forever frozen into picturesque attitudes for the benefit of the tour groups. So, like everyone else, sooner or later they have got to take their chance. One can only hope that the inevitable far-reaching changes will come gradually and in a form that the islanders can digest without distorting their personalities or the ancient structure of their society.

10 Do It Yourself

Before you can do anything yourself with shells, it is first necessary to clean them, and if you have ever tried the operation, the problem will be appreciated. However, to every sheller on this earth it cometh soon or late. There are nine different ways of cleaning them, the most satisfactory of which is to get someone else to do it. This method should be employed on the spot, where such natural aids as brine, sand, and ants abound to help the selected guide, fisherman, or beachcomber in his task. He should be sternly supervised. All too often, on delivering your catch to you, he will demand a heavy fee for his pains. Actually, he has stuffed cotton wool up the creature's whorl to contain the stench, which presently manifests itself with intensified pungency.

The other cleaning techniques to be used in situ are those of (a) boiling, (b) freezing, (c) burying, (d) scouring, and (e) hanging; and I shall describe these processes in that order.

Live mollusks should be steeped in tepid water and brought slowly to a boil in order not to crack the glossy surface of the shell. Leave them to simmer for about ten minutes and let them cool off before attempting to extract the creature with eyebrow or other tweezers.

To freeze mollusks, put them in the lower part of the refrigerator for two hours, then transfer them to the freezer and leave them there for three days. Then reverse the process.

214

Finally, soak them in cold water after which remove the animal as before.

When it comes to burying shells in hot sand in order that the flesh may be eaten by ants, it is desirable to remember where you have put them. Personally, I have never stayed anywhere long enough for this system to be successful, but I can appreciate the simplicity of the method if your life is passed in some marine paradise. In this case, it is as well to bury the shells some distance from the house and to leeward. It will take the ants a month to discharge their duties.

The practice of scouring in bathrooms has usually been our portion, as stoves and refrigerators are not readily accessible in tourist hotels. We soak the shells overnight in cold fresh water. With luck the mollusk will unlock its doors in death if it is a bivalve, or if a univalve it sometimes, though seldom, partially emerges. The former is easy to clean once you have grasped, so to speak, the nettle. If not already open, the bivalve can be pried apart with a sharp knife, the creature scooped out, cast away, and the plug pulled on it. It is the univalve that foxes you. At the first touch it is liable to withdraw to the summit or apex of its whorl and there, odoriferously and inaccessibly, to perish. It takes weeks, sometimes months, to dislodge it, piece by piece.

This introduces the topic of hanging, the last of the first group of alternatives. This effective but unattractive method was practiced daily by Bobby, our mentor in Mauritius. He would insert a fishhook attached to a strong lever through the aperture of the shell into the creature's flesh and hang it on a clothesline in full sun. The animal, gradually weakening and uncoiling, usually on the third day would shed its shell on the grass, and be left pendant in all its nakedness. Bobby's backyard was a sorry sight. It reminded me of Gethsemane or Tyburn, and I avoided it.

The only commercial seller with whom we have been on close terms, and who divulged her tactics to us in detail, was a Mrs. Turk on Marco Island. In her back garden she had a tub filled with a 50 percent solution of chlorine bleach, into which she

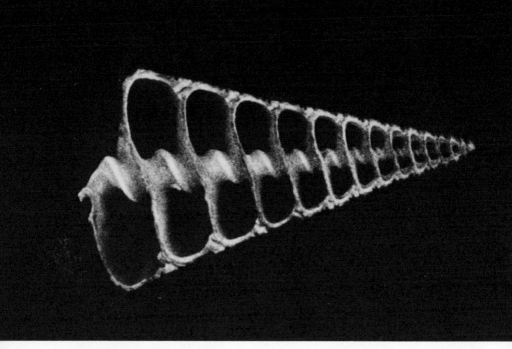

It is the univalve that foxes you. It is liable to withdraw to the summit or apex of its whorl and there, odoriferously and inaccessibly, to perish. Photograph by Sara Heaton.

plunged the harvest as it came in from the beachcombers on the Florida Keys. This liquid pickles the flesh and also dislodges obstinate growths of barnacles from the surface as if by magic. Many shells are encrusted with white lime, and this Mrs. Turk removed by soaking them in hydrochloric acid, finishing them off by hand with a surgical scalpel. After this drastic treatment they would be buffed on a circular electrical polisher to restore the gloss. No one but Mr. Cooper, the bulb grower of Maui, has ever suggested the use of a meat tenderizer. Perhaps it doesn't work.

Let us now assume that you have reached your native shore with a cargo of decomposing mollusks. Fortunately, you are unlikely to meet again your neighbors in the plane, who have been forced to endure the journey in an ever-increasing atmosphere of putrefaction. If you live in restricted conditions,

in a terrace house perhaps, or in an apartment, practical difficulties are likely to hamper the fulfillment of the next three
techniques. These difficulties are associated with plumbing, with
a dearth of durable vessels, and with the lack of a bathtub at
the bottom of the garden. For bleaches corrode, acids erode,
and the fumes of ethyl alcohol (warmly recommended by many
malocologists) make you feel tight. However, the text books
on conchology all insist that your mollusks should be (a)
pickled in isopropyl alcohol or (b) be purged à la Madame
Turk in chlorine or (c) be supersaturated in a saline solution,
with a view to extracting the creature whole with forceps when
the moment is ripe. So take your pick. Beware, however, of
burning off a finger or two. Be careful not to melt the lavatory
basin. Take care not to dissolve the metal pipes of your plumbing. Be sure not to burn holes in your clothes or in the linoleum. If the fumes induce semi- or total blindness, call the
doctor. In other words you are okay if you have access to a
well-equipped laboratory. Otherwise not.

I mentioned in the opening chapter that I owned a studio
in which I made shell pictures but did not disclose that I had
given a one-man exhibition of them in London and subsequently
showed them in other salons in the West End, as well as in
Brighton and in Portmeirion. I was greatly struck by the keen
interest shown by the purchasers in exactly how the pictures
were made. Perhaps they bought them to find out. Anyway, I
propose to describe the process in detail, but before doing so
to give an account of the exhibtion and of the events leading
up to it.

"But what will you do with all these shells?" our household
used to exclaim in dismay when, weighed down with newspaper
parcels and bulging native baskets, we would be washed up on
our own doorstep looking like a couple of refugees. They also
seemed disturbed at the thought of our bill for overweight. This
item was a new experience for Pat. In the days of his "Florida
only" collection, he was accustomed to return home with a
dozen or so shells in his spongebag, having thrown away all
those that did not surpass in perfection the ones already in his

217

Collection of miniature shells (with one cowry on top to show the scale) in eighteenth-century collector's cabinet. Photograph by Sara Heaton.

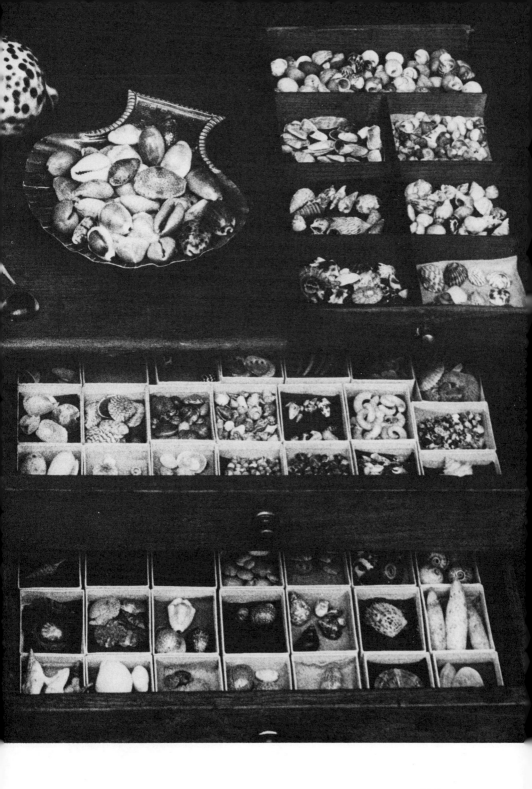

coffee table in Buffalo. From the start my reaction had been entirely different. I longed to create something from the less-than-perfect specimens, but as yet had no idea what. I used to stand on the beach entranced by the patterns of shells, starfish, and sea wrack, which the movement of the waves traced on the sand. "If only," I would think, "I could take these home exactly as they lie, what a gorgeous picture they would make!" It was not long before I realized that I could take them

The early shell pictures were made in conditions of such discomfort for everyone that it quickly became apparent that I had to find a studio. Photograph by Patrick Hodgson.

home. Whether I could do as good a job as the sea in making them into a picture had yet to be seen. So after we got back the best specimens were syphoned off for the museum, some duplicates were set aside for collector friends and, of course, for the children, while the rest were assembled in piles on a card table.

The early shell pictures were made in conditions of such discomfort for everyone that it quickly became apparent that

Submarine Garden by Martha Hodgson.

I had to find a studio, and I was lucky indeed to get one close by. These first pictures consisted of scatterings of beachcombing mounted on a sand-colored background. They bore such titles as *Low Tide at Captiva* (or Marco, or Coconut Island), *Submarine Garden, Rip Tide, Tide Race* or *Spring on the Ocean Bed.* Their effectiveness quite startled me. A sort of pressure from within began to make itself felt as brainwaves crowded into my mind, clamoring for expression through the shells. Inspiration sprang at me from all directions. A Dutch flower painting in the Victoria and Albert, an Adam ceiling at Kenwood in Hampstead, a Chinese plate at Sotheby's, a morning glory on my balcony, a wheat field seen from a train, an oak in Hurstbourne Park. Next my imagination turned compulsively back to the beaches from which I had drawn my material, and primitive scenes with names such as *Marco Remembered, April at Coon Key, White Heat,* and *Peach Farm Bay* came into being. Their naïve strength took me by surprise, and a number of them were most imaginatively framed by a man in Battersea Rise who has since become a monk. It was not long until over thirty pictures hung on my walls, unseen by any eyes except my own, and I began to wonder what on earth to do with them. But new ideas continued to press upward and outward, and each week produced a fresh crop of pictures.

222

Summer on the Ocean Bed by Martha Hodgson.

At about this stage two incidents took place simultaneously. Some close friends of ours, Ward and Ella Foshay, arrived in London, and under the influence of a good dinner I invited them and Pat over to my studio. Ella is not one to beat about the bush. "Are these for sale?" she asked. I supposed they were. All I knew for certain was I needed more space. She bought three on the spot and bore them off to New York. The second event was the private view at the Upper Grosvenor Gallery of some paintings by an old Roedean friend of mine known as Pig.[1] Pig has a fascinating and complex personality; she is a mystic, a superb cook, a fine artist, and chairman of the map publishers, Geographers'. The minute I entered the gallery I felt that sense of inevitability that often precedes some critical encounter with one's own destiny. I quickly discovered, however, that the Upper Grosvenor Gallery, in the shape of its owner, the duchess of St. Albans, did not think in terms of exhibitions of shell collages. Her former exhibitors had included such artists as Dame Laura Knight, Augustus John, Pietro Annigoni, Sir Frank Brangwyn, and James Fitton, and only after considerable pressure could I persuade the duchess even to visit my studio. But six months later an exhibition, firmly backed by Trenchard Cox [2] and David Carritt [3] staggered off the ground in her gallery, at which were sold over fifty pictures to a cross section of shell fanciers. These ranged from the Queen Mother to a shorthand typist, who "wanted something beautiful for her basement bedsitter"; from the chairman of the Shell Oil Company for the hall of his skyscraper on South Bank to Agatha Christie and her husband, Max; from Lee Radziwell to one of the Rolling Stones (which one I cannot say due to his curtain of hair). I also did a picture for Ted Heath of his ill-fated *Morning Cloud,* using a marlin bone for the sail of the yacht.

When the Queen Mother arrived, she was wearing a gentian blue soufflé of a hat exactly matching the color of her eyes. She showed an instant appreciation of the spell cast by the shell, and confided that she kept a bowl in the hall of the Castle of Mey into which she dropped her finds after her daily walk on the beach. She bought a Dutch flower picture and a Valentine done in her racing colors.

"Tell me, why is that one called *Design for Jane's Bathroom?*" the Queen Mother presently asked, stopping before a formal design of white pectens. I explained that my sister-in-law, Jane, had remarked that my pictures were "very adequate for a bathroom."

[1] Phyllis Pearsall.
[2] Sir Trenchard Cox, late keeper of the Victoria & Albert Museum.
[3] Expert on old master paintings and consultant to Christie's.

Exhibition of shell collages, called "Coquillages," at Upper Grosvenor Galleries, London. David Carritt (with Martha Hodgson) per-
forms the opening ceremony. Photograph by Patrick Hodgson.

"Good gracious!" exclaimed the Queen Mother. "I've got a sister-in-law like that too. I hope you haven't given her one."

The unexpected success of this exhibition aroused the interest not only of Her Majesty but of Her Majesty's inland revenue inspector, a figure I had not previously associated with the fruits of beachcombing. Succor was extended by my tax advisers in the shape of a thin young accountant. He blew in out of a snowstorm and sat on the edge of a chair in my drawing room muffled in an overcoat dotted with snowflakes the size of Smarties, an anxious character in thick spectacles clasping a dispatch case. It became immediately apparent that he had done a beautiful job, reducing a stock of incoherent notes and bills to a pithily expressed statement, laid out in a numerical design as graceful and lucid as a parabola.

I experienced a rush of admiration. "Did you do these accounts?" He flushed. "Yes."

"But they are beautiful! How could you boil all that down to just this?"

A beam of merriment illuminated his eye and he made a modest movement of repudiation.

"I do think you should see what these figures represent. Would you like to see our shells?"

Confronted by the shells—burnished, gleaming, streamlined— he reacted rather like a baby boy on a beach with a bucket.

"But they're *fabulous*. They are wonderful." He turned quite pink. "How do these get such a high polish?"

"The shell's covered all the time by a protective mantle that is only withdrawn when it's in danger."

"How do you mean, mantle? Is it some kind of animal orgasm?"

Certainly it's not that. Supposing him to mean organism, I decided not to pursue this train of thought.

"These are from Fiji; these from Mexico; those below come from East Africa; and the ones on the top shelves from the Cayman Islands and West Florida. Bali, the Scillies, Herm, North Borneo, and the Mediterranean are in these drawers."

There are three tables in my studio that are arranged in the figure of a U, so that, by sitting at the base on the inside,

I am encircled by the materials and tools I need to make my pictures. It is a good idea for the beginner to start off by visiting a do-it-yourself shop and to lay in a selection of boards in different sizes on which to make the pictures. The most effective proportion I find is a multiple of the classical 2 x 3, but I also have squares, long panels, and a few ovals; the latter, although attractive, are not practical because of the heavy expense of framing them. Chipboard or plywood are both good buys, or if you want to use the grain of wood as a background, which will look like sand, ask for reeded hardboard. I buy French felt for covering the boards, since the felt marries well with the glue and holds the shells securely in place. French felt is superior in texture and sharper in color than English felt and therefore more effective, but it is not always easy to find. Sam Beasley, at the Portmeirrion shop in Pont Street, has a marvelous range, and I get mine there. But velvet, silk, wall-paper, or any other fabric that pleases you would do equally well.

Place the board on the material and draw around it with a piece of dressmaker's chalk to get the right size. Cover the board with an even coat of paste, such as Sobo or Copydex. Don't forget to give the bottle a good shake and put the cap on after use. Cut out the material and ease it onto the board, smoothing it before you to avoid air bubbles. Place the board face down, put a weight on it . . . and leave it overnight to dry.

In the meantime you will have conceived some mental image of the picture you want to make, so assemble around you all the materials you need, as well as tools like forceps, scissors, a knife, a tape measure, chalk, etc., in order that your inspiration may not dry up while you search madly for the glue.

Glue. This is most important. I was in despair until I found Uhu, which is colorless, sticks instantly, and holds forever. Thus you can work fast while the mood is on you, as if you were drawing, and there is none of that frustration of waiting for the glue to become tacky. I simply dip my shell into the glue and stick it straight on to the picture.

Let us assume, for example, that you have decided to make a flower picture. Having visualized the whole thing in your mind's eye, start with the vase. Do not put it too near the edge, for the frame will reduce the size of your background. It is a common mistake not to leave enough margin around your subject. Having completed the vase, next stick on the stems of the flowers, which may be made from seaweed, sea oats, sea fern, or possibly even from wire. (I sometimes use Japanese radio wire.) Before starting on the flowers themselves, I always put a board with a weight on it over the stalks to ensure that they dry flat, and again leave it over night.

When it comes to making the flowers and foliage, it is necessary to go cautiously. Leaves are a constant difficulty, as only the mussel shell and some opercula are leaf-shaped. I get a jeweler to cut a section of certain shells with a circular saw, which proves to be a good solution. Next I lay the shells in position on the board, moving them round to balance the color and shape of the shells and the general design of the picture. Occasionally I stick down one key shell when I am certain it is correctly positioned, and work from that point, gradually building up the whole. Often I leave a picture half-finished that I may see it with a fresh eye in the morning. When it is completed I put it on a shelf opposite my bed so that it is the first thing I see on waking. It is surprising how clearly the faults stand out. "It needs a little more on the top left" for instance, or "It's too heavy in the center."

I personally think it spoils shell pictures to apply any tinting or varnish whatsoever. Also, it is important to frame the pictures with imagination. Although the frame for obvious reasons has to be of the box type, the picture must not look boxed in. Since the medium is a heavy one, an effect of lightness and space should be aimed at. For this reason the surround of the frame should be sloping and not set at right angles.

As in any other form of art, only practical hints can be passed on from one fabricator of shell pictures to another. There is no known secret of how to make them acceptable— it is a matter of relationship between the material, in this case the shell, and the handler of it. It either works or it doesn't. It will please some but not others. Every coastal town in Florida has its shell shop, most of which sell equipment for making shell pictures and conduct classes for those who buy their materials there. And Florida abounds with stupifyingly hideous shell pictures and so-called works of art, sprayed, enameled, and embellished with spangles, beads, plastic, and coy little figures.

Repulsive shell pictures are among the least of the misfortunes that have overtaken Florida. The sparse simplicity of the mangrove swamps and the bird-haunted plains of saw grass have given way to the building boom, the petrol pump, and the billboard. Even nature has inflicted a wound of its own, for lately the shores of the west coast have been bedevilled every few years by the disastrous "red tide," which stains the ocean a deep salmon pink, while the water becomes heavy and oily to the touch. Mollusca and fish perish by the million, the glassy

I found four of the treasures of Florida for which I have been searching for years: the junonia at Marco; a lemon pecten at Boca Grande; on the same beach, a coal black fan shell; and at Siesta Key a lion's paw. Photograph by Sara Heaton.

surface of the sea is pricked over with their upturned bellies and tails and the channels choked with their bodies, which presently pile themselves odoriferously on the beaches. In 1947 one of these tides is said to have killed upward of fifty million creatures of the sea, and it can readily be imagined that it has taken years for the different species to have reasserted themselves. This year the islands of Sanibel, Captiva, and Boca Grande were all suffering the aftermath of one of these visitations, but no one on the spot seemed able to account for its cause. Through an expert on plankton in the Conchological Society, I have discovered that what sparks off a red tide is an abnormal percentage of a minute organism called the dinoflagellates, which overbreeds in the sea when it exceeds its normal temperature. The Red Sea is so called because this condition is chronic there. The water becomes red and slimy because it contains millions of these creatures to every pint.

We have just now returned from what I suppose will be our last shell expedition to Florida or probably anywhere else. Our collection, which must now number over ten thousand, does not need fresh shells; it needs to be digested, rearranged, and catalogued. Besides, on this last visit, in spite of the red tide, I found four of the treasures of Florida for which I have been searching for years: the junonia at Marco, the finding of which I have already described; a lemon pecten at Boca Grande, so yellow that I nearly passed it over thinking it was a plastic bottle top and, on the same beach, a coal black fan shell. Very rare. At Siesta Key I found a lion's paw, a pecten so desirable that I had already bought one for Pat, thinking never to find one ourselves. Clutching this treasure I raced home to show it to my brother Terry, and during my absence one of a pair of my yellow shoes was carried away on the rising tide. Four days later the sea returned the shoe to the beach at exactly the point from which it had been taken. Fate seems unlikely to surpass itself in granting greater benedictions than all these, and I am inclined to think the moment has come to bow out of the arena while I can still bow at all, for bending these days is becoming increasingly difficult.

Appendix

OF COMMON AND LATIN NAMES
OF SHELLS DESCRIBED IN THIS BOOK

A
Abalone, red: *Haliotis rufescens*
        green: *Haliotis fulgens*
Angel's wing: *Cyrtopleura costata*
Apple murex: *Murex pomum*
Ark shells: *Arcidae*
Auger shells: *Terebridae*
Auger screw turret: *Turritella terebra*
Aulicus cone: *Conus aulicus*

B
Bailer: *Melo aethiopicus*
Banded tulip: *Fasciolaria tulipa*
Black olive: *Oliva oliva*
Bleeding tooth nerite: *Nerita peloronta*
Boat shell: *Crepidula fornicata*
Broken heart cockle: *Corculum cardissa*
Bubble shell: *Haminoea elegans*
Buttercup: *Anodontia alba*

C
Cabbage murex: *Murex brassica*
Caribbean land snail: *Euglandina rosea*
Cat's paw: *Plicatula gibbosa*
Chambered nautilus: *Nautilus pompilius*
Checkerboard clam: *Macrocallista maculata*

THE SPELL OF THE SHELL

Chinese alphabet cone: *Conus spurius atlanticus*
Chiton: *Guildingia obtecta*
Cobalt blue (Yasawa Isles): *Linkia*
Comb Venus: *Pitar lupanaria*
Coquina: *Donax variabilis*
Crown of thorns (Pacific): *Acanthaster laevigata*
Cup-and-saucer limpet: *Calyptraea chinensis*

D
Dawn cowry: *Cypraea diluculum*
Distorted cowry: *Cypraea moneta* rostrée
Duck foot: *Aporrhais occidentalis*

E
Egg cowry: *Ovula ovum*
Elegant disk: *Dosinia elegans*
Elegant Venus: *Pitar dione*
Episcopal miter: *Mitra mitra*
Eyed cowry: *Cypraea argus*

F
Fan shell: Upper valve of *Pectinidae*
Fighting conch: *Strombus pugilis*
Flamingo tongue: *Cyphoma gibbosum*

G
Geographic cone: *Conus geographus*
Giant clam: *Tridacna gigas*
Glory of Bengal: *Conus bengalensis*
Glory of the sea: *Conus gloriamaris*
Gold ring cowry: *Cypraea annulus*
Golden cowry: *Cypraea aurantium*
Goose barnacle: *Lepas anatifera*

H
Hebrew cone: *Conus ebraeus*
Helmet (Bull-mouthed): *Cypraecassis rufa*
Horse conch: *Fasciolaria gigantea*
Humpback cowry: *Cypraea mauritiana*

I

Imperial harp: *Harpa costata*
Imperial volute: *Voluta imperialis*
Isabel's cowry: *Cypraea isabella*

J

Jingle shell: *Anomia simplex*
Junonia: *Scaphella junonia*

K

Kinoshitai's latiaxis: *Latiaxis kinashitai*

L

Lady's (or old maid's) curl: *Vermicularia spirata*
Lady's ear or ear shell: *Sinum perspectivum*
Land snail: *Achatina fulica*
Lemon pecten: *Chlamys gloriosus*
Lettered cone: *Conus litteratus*
Lettered olive: *Oliva sayana*
Lightning conch: *Busycon perversum*
Lightning whelk: *Busycon contrarium*
Limpet: *Patella vulgata*
Lion's paw: *Lyropecten nodosus*
Little jewel box: *Chama sarda*

M

Magpie shell: *Cittarium pica*
Map cowry: *Cypraea mappa*
Miter shells: *Mitridae*
Mole cowry: *Cypraea talpa*
Money cowry: *Cypraea moneta*
Mussel: *Choromytilus chorus*

Nutmeg: *Cancellaria reticulata*
Niger cowry: *Cypraea eglantina niger*

O

Olive turban: *Astraea olivacea*
Omaria cone: *Conus omaria*

Onion tun: *Tonna allium*
Orange-mouthed olive: *Oliva sericea*
Ormer shell: *Haliotis fulgens*
Oysters: *Ostreidae*

P
Paper bubble: *Haminoea crocata*
Paper fig shell: *Ficus communis*
Paper nautilus: *Argonauta argo*
Pearl trigonia: *Neotrigonia margaritacea*
Pearly top: *Trochus niloticus*
Ponderous ark: *Noetia ponderosa*
Purple dye shell: *"Murex purpura"*

R
Reticulated cowry: *Cypraea maculifera*
Rose petal: *Tellina lineata*

S
Sand dollar: *Echinarachnius parma*
Scallop, bay: *Argopecten irradians*
          ornate: *Chlamys ornatus*
          rough: *Aequipecten muscocus*
Scarlet (Mauritius): *Oreasteridae*
Scorpion conch: *Lambis scorpius*
Scotch bonnet: *Phalium granulatum*
Sea anemone: *Actiniaria*
Serpent's head cowry: *Cypraea caputserpentis*
Spider conch: *Lambis lambis*
Spindle shell: *Tibia fusus*
Star shell: *Stellaria solaris*
Starfish: *Asteroidea*
Sunrise tellin: *Tellina radiata*
Sundial: *Architectonica granulata*

T
Tapestry turban: *Turbo petholatus*
Telescope shell: *Telescopium telescopium*
Tent olive: *Oliva porphyria*

234

Tessellata cowry: *Cypraea tesselata*
Textile cone: *Conus textile*
Thorny oyster: *Spondylus americanus*
Thorny scallop: *Chlamys sentis*
Tiger cowry: *Cypraea tigris*
Triton's trumpet: *Charonia tritonis*
Tulip cone: *Conus tulipa*
Tulip shell: *Fasciolaria tulipa*
Turkey wing: *Arca zebra*

V
Ventricose harp: *Harpa major*
Venus' comb murex: *Murex pecten*
Violet sea snail: *Janthina janthina*
Violet spider conch: *Lambis violacea*
Virgin cone: *Conus virgo*
Van Gogh: *Heliasteridae*

W
Wing shell: *Pholas campechiensis*

Z
Zebra top shell: *Trochus niloticus*

Index